Essay on Human Reason

On the Principle of Identity and Difference

Nikola Stojkoski

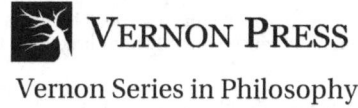

Vernon Series in Philosophy

Copyright © 2019 Vernon Press, an imprint of Vernon Art and Science Inc, on behalf of the author.

All rights reserved. No part of this publication may be reproduced, stored in a retrieval system, or transmitted in any form or by any means, electronic, mechanical, photocopying, recording, or otherwise, without the prior permission of Vernon Art and Science Inc.

www.vernonpress.com

In the Americas:
Vernon Press
1000 N West Street,
Suite 1200, Wilmington,
Delaware 19801
United States

In the rest of the world:
Vernon Press
C/Sancti Espiritu 17,
Malaga, 29006
Spain

Series in Philosophy

Library of Congress Control Number: 2018931472

ISBN: 978-1-62273-492-4

Product and company names mentioned in this work are the trademarks of their respective owners. While every care has been taken in preparing this work, neither the authors nor Vernon Art and Science Inc. may be held responsible for any loss or damage caused or alleged to be caused directly or indirectly by the information contained in it.

Every effort has been made to trace all copyright holders, but if any have been inadvertently overlooked the publisher will be pleased to include any necessary credits in any subsequent reprint or edition.

Table of Contents

Introduction vii

1. Reason as a cognitive subject 1
  1.1 It is all in our heads 1
  1.2 What is a thing? 9
    1.2.1 What is a particular thing? 10
    1.2.2 What is a universal thing? 12
  1.3 Knowledge of sensations – where the material touches the mental 14
    1.3.1 Heartcore 17
    1.3.2 On the difference between being and non-being 19
    1.3.3 On the quantitative relation between reality as we know it and reality in itself 21
    1.3.4 Problem of justification 22
  1.4 Cognition of perceptions 27
  1.5 Cognition of universals 31

2. Reason as a thinking subject 35
  2.1 Induction 35
  2.2 Deduction 37
  2.3 Analogy 40
  2.4 Analysis 44
  2.5 Association 48
  2.6 Abstraction 53
  2.7 Generalization 54
  2.8 Categorization 55
  2.9 Definition 55

3. Reason as a logical subject – truth   59
    3.1 Truth is an identity relation   60
    3.2 Correspondence   60
    3.3 Sketch of an alternative theory of truth   62
       3.3.1 Relation between independent reality as we know it and dependent reality as we know it   63
          Locke's Argument   65
          Hume's Argument   66
          Givenness Criteria Argument   66
          On Objectivity as a Universal Consent   68
          Illusions and Hallucinations   69
       3.3.2 Three types of truth   70

4. Reason as an aesthetical subject – beauty   73
    4.1 Classical theory of beauty   73
    4.2 Analysis of aesthetical categories   77
    4.3 Enslaving of the muses   83
    4.4 Ontology of beauty   85
       4.4.1 The 'hard' meaning of distinction   85
       4.4.2 The 'soft' meaning of distinction   86

5. Reason as a moral subject – goodness   91
    5.1 Equality is the essence of morality   91
    5.2 Justice   97
    5.3 Golden rule of ethics   101
    5.4 Categorical imperative   102
    5.5 Analysis of ethical categories   103
    5.6 On the problem of justification or the source of morality   106

Philosophical Monolith   111

Bibliography   117

Index   123

To those who can, without being entranced, plunge into the great abyss

Introduction

Dear reader, a certain pattern in the functioning of the human reason has been noticed which shows itself again and again on the examination on each separate appearance of reason. You will be acquainted with it in the pages to follow. On the basis of this 'pattern', an attempt will be made to answer the question how does the reason work and to derive its definition from there.

Reason has indirectly been the subject of study almost through the entire history of philosophy, with various individual appearances of the reason being most often the subject of philosophical investigation. By taking a step back, this work makes reason, in general, its subject of investigation and makes an attempt at comprehending its essence. What is the reason? According to its contemporary definitions, it is "the power of the mind to think, understand, and form judgements logically"[1] or simply as "the sum of the intellectual powers."[2] Ayn Rand defines reason as "the faculty that identifies and integrates the material provided by man's senses" (Rand, 1964, 14) with it emphasizing also its cognitive function. The term 'reason' will be understood here in its broadest sense where the sum of the intellectual powers, aside from the cognitive function, also incorporates the power to cognize beauty, as well as the power to act in moral ways. In any case, it cannot be said that these and other existing definitions completely satisfy my philosophical curiosity because they simply inform about what the reason does and not the ways in which it does it.

In Western philosophy, reason is an essential property of man, their *differentia specifica* and privilege. It is the most complex ability a being can have considering its place of residence – the brain, which is the most complex material structure, therefore, the aim of this work – comprehending its essence – is, accordingly, extremely immodest. It is certain that the ultimate knowledge – what reason is in general sense – according to its definition, breezes through each separate appearance of reason. If it

---

[1] "reason, n." *OED Online*, Oxford University Press, June 2017, https://en.oxforddictionaries.com/definition/reason. Accessed 24 December 2017.

[2] Reason. (n.d.). Retrieved January 15, 2016, from <http://www.merriam-webster.com/dictionary/reason>

is present in each separate appearance of reason, then the ultimate knowledge is what is common for all – from the simplest to the most complex – appearances of reason. Searching for the common in countless different appearances of reason would be a remarkably extensive and practically impossible task. However, this task will be simplified for the purpose of this work by using the fact that the vast number of various appearances of reason is categorized under several general areas in philosophy.

I will move inductively, separately analyzing five of the most general forms of reason existence, in order to reach the sought after generalization in the end. The first appearance of reason which will be scrutinized is the cognitive process of objective reality where an attempt will be made to explain the manner in which reason processes material provided by the senses to create the things we know and these are the individual sensations, perceptions, and in the end – the universals. Here a new, alternative theory of knowledge will be offered, inspired by and based on a possible answer to the old metaphysical question – what is a thing. It can be said that all remaining conclusions are based on the theory of knowledge, as the most fundamental of philosophical disciplines, according to many – with greater depth than ontology. The second appearance of reason which will be examined is the thinking, considering the most important operations of the reason known under the common name – abstract logical reasoning. The next subject of analysis will be the nature of truth as a central logical category. Here an answer to the question 'what is the truth' will be offered, resulting in a new metaphysics along with possible solutions to the ontological status of truth-bearers and truth-makers. This will be followed by the investigation of reason as an aesthetical subject where the nature and origin of beauty will be analyzed. Based on this analysis surfaces the answer to the dilemma of objectivity and subjectivity in beauty. The appearances of reason as a moral subject are the final topic where I will deal with another old metaphysical question – what is goodness. Based on the possible answer to this question I will attempt to ground morality while offering solutions to the metaethical problems related to the justification and foundation of moral judgments.

Thus considered forms of reason existence are so general that they as a whole contain almost the entire reason activity. As it can be noted, fundamental philosophical disciplines are considered, such as the theory of knowledge, logic, aesthetics, and ethics. What is common for them is that they are all products of the reason and only the principle in which the reason functions is the principle which will unite everything.

Through these analyses, I will try to prove that if we go deep enough, each appearance of reason can be reduced to a same common core. The common core which all these reason forms of existence reduce to is the identification and differentiation. Everything the reason does, all its functions in its immense diversity, is reduced to two basic operations: identification and differentiation. Each activity of the reason, regardless of its kind and level of complexity, is a combination of miniature atom-like identifications and differentiations. Therefore, I will try to defend a bold thesis that reason functions on the principle of identity and difference, i.e. that it is an ability to identify and differentiate. With this, I will try to describe a very strong and clear relationship between ethics, aesthetics, logic, epistemology, and all other appearances of reason out of the scope of these philosophical disciplines which here fuse into one. Dear reader, finally, before you is an attempt of the reason to explain reason, to explain itself, elevating itself to a higher level of self-awareness.

****

This book is an original monograph. It is translated from Macedonian by Dragana Velkovska.

1.
Reason as a cognitive subject

The first appearance of reason which will be considered here is cognition. We acquire knowledge of the world through the cognitive process using reason. Cognition is one of the fundamental appearances and functions of reason and the subject of study of epistemology. The most specific definition of epistemology or the theory of knowledge, as it is also called, is the study of knowledge. Knowledge usually means knowledge of propositions, however, I here will delve a little bit deeper and above all will deal with the knowledge of things themselves. I consider knowledge of things more fundamental than knowledge of propositions because things are their constituents and with that their knowledge is a necessary precondition for knowledge of the propositions.

In this chapter, first will be presented the initial ontological – gnoseological assumptions upon which an attempt will be made to build a new solution to the problem of knowledge. Then, the answer to the old metaphysical question – What is a thing, follows. This answer is the foundation of the theory set forth here; the defining of the nature of things will allow us to reflect on the way of their creation because each creation carries with itself information on the manner of its creating. Further, the topic of discussion will be the way of acquiring knowledge of sensations, perceptions, and in the end the universals, according to a unique principle that unites them all. From the presented solution of the problem of knowledge, interesting consequences result which will be analyzed at the end of the chapter and which relate to the problem of the non-being, the relation between reality as we know it and reality in itself, as well as the problem of justifying our beliefs of reality in itself.

1.1 It is all in our heads

The entire theory presented here, in the manner of naturalized epistemology, is built on the foundation of a causal sequence confirmed in the natural sciences which relates to the cognitive process. The firmness of this foundation comes from the firmness and reliability of scientific methods. The cognitive function of man is subject to an investigation of modern psychology, cognitive science, neuroscience, and other related scientific disciplines. All of these agree that the cognitive process happens in the following causal sequence: first of all, light, sound, and other external world signals reach our sensory organs. Sensory organs turn light, sound, and the rest of the sensory signals into electric impulses suitable to be processed by reason. These electrical impulses through the nerve pathways arrive in the brain which is the material carrier of reason. After they reach the brain, the processing of the electrical impulses by the reason begins, and as a result, we obtain sensations, perceptions, or content of sensory experience in general.[1] The manner of processing of the electrical impulses, which is one of the greatest mysteries of philosophy and science in general, is the main target of this chapter.[2]

First of all, based on this causal sequence I will arrive at several conclusions which will be useful to set the scene for a new insight into the problem of knowledge. These conclusions relate to the object and subject of cognition, to the sources of knowledge, and the distinction between reality in itself and reality as we know it.

What can be concluded?

1. From the fact that our sensory organs are reached by light, sound, and other signals from the outside world, one can conclude that there is an objective reality existing outside and independently of our reason and will. Contrary to this, there are opposing views in philosophy, such as subjective realism, for example, that reject the existence of objective reality. According to them, there is only reason and its ideas. However absurd, each theoretical attempt to refute the thesis that external reality does not exist, it has the counterargument that each theoretical attempt presupposes the existence of reason (subject) that theorizes, and with that the possibility of the existence of the Descartes' demon that deceives us. Consciousness can never be transcended. Kant calls this vicious cycle, the inability to prove the existence of the external world, 'Scandal of Philosophy.'[3] We are therefore left with the choice to accept this initial ontological principle as a self-evident and intuitive truth, merely as a belief, with no proof.

2. The sensory organs are the source of knowledge of the outside world. They provide the sensory material from which the reason creates

---

[1] See *Principles of Neural Science* (Kandel, et all., 2000, chap. 21, p. [411-412]) or especially the conclusion, page 428.
[2] With these, relatively new, scientific notions, we have a certain advantage compared to classical philosophers which investigated the problem of knowledge.
[3] See Preface to Second Edition, *Critique of Pure Reason*, Bxl, p.121.

knowledge. Contrary to this, in philosophy one often comes across the view that the source of knowledge is the sensory experience. Namely, two opposing views are known in philosophy relating to the question of the sources of knowledge – empiricism and rationalism. General view of empiricism is that the sensory experience is the ultimate source of our knowledge, while the general view of rationalism is that reason is a primary source of knowledge and that there is knowledge which we come across independently of our sensory experience. Both acknowledge sensory experience as a source of knowledge, but "The dispute between rationalism and empiricism concerns the extent to which we are dependent upon sensory experience in our effort to gain knowledge" (Markie, entry).

The conception of experience is problematic, to say the least. "Experience is easily thought of as a stream of private events, known only to their possessor..." (Blackburn, 1996). This stream of events has its contents: "... experiences have contents: it is the world itself that they represent to us as being one way or another..." (ibid). The contents presuppose the existence of things, and the existence of things means that we already have knowledge of them. In fact, the very definition confirms that in our experience we already have knowledge of events – "known only to their possessor". Once we already have knowledge in experience, I consider it a mistake to determine this experience as a source of knowledge.

Also, British empiricists John Locke, George Berkeley, and David Hume "...maintained that all knowledge is obtained through sensory experience—from what we see, hear, feel, taste, and smell" (Kandel et al., 2000, Chap. 21, p. [412]). Sensory experience is what we see, hear, taste, and smell. What we see, hear, feel taste, and smell are the colors, sounds, tastes, and smells. They are perceptions – things that are segments of space or time. The existence of these things in our experience as its contents, the awareness of them, however elementary they may be, means that we do have the knowledge of those things. The experience of the red color of the apple already represents knowledge of the color of the apple. Therefore I consider it a mistake to claim that experience is the source of knowledge. The source should be sought somewhere deeper.

'Sensory experience' to me is a totality of sensations and perceptions from which the knowledge of propositions stems, and according to this when it is claimed that the source of the knowledge is a sensory experience above all, a knowledge of propositions is in fact what it is meant. Propositions are knowledge about things, and they presuppose knowledge of things themselves because things are constituents of propositions. However, here, as it was already mentioned in the introduction, it is not meant knowledge of propositions, but, above all, knowledge of things themselves and this is why I cannot agree with this generally accepted epistemological view. As it was already mentioned above, I consider sensations and perceptions already acquired knowledge and accordingly it cannot be said that they are the source of knowledge. On the contrary, there is a need to define the source of their knowledge. Therefore, I will take a step back into the field of experimental psychology and neuroscience and say that the source of knowledge of sensations and perceptions are the sensory organs that provide reason with electrical impulses which serve as sensory material.[4]

3. Among other things, the objective reality existing outside and independently of our reason appears as an object of sensory cognition.[5] This is a common materialistic or realistic thesis, as it is known in the theory of knowledge, which is accepted even in natural sciences.

On the other hand, different theses for the object of cognition are known in philosophy according to which this object has a non-material nature. One such popular view is in the theory of perception, also known as 'sense-datum theory', where sensations and perceptions, or sense-data as they are called there, are considered objects of the sensory experience. There are many versions of this theory. Idealist versions which "deny that we are aware of mind-independent objects at all, directly or indirectly, but only of sense-data" (Crane, para. 3.1.1) we simply reject, among other things, as incompatible with neuroscience and naturalism in general.

One version, however, that is arguably compatible with the science of perception, is the indirect realism or representative realism, as it is also called: „The sense-datum theory can say, however, that we are indirectly aware of ordinary objects: that is, aware of them by being aware of sense-data. A sense-datum theorist who says this is known as an indirect realist

---

[4] "In each sensory system the initial contact with the external world occurs through specialized neural structures called sensory receptors. The sensory receptor is the first cell in each sensory pathway and transforms stimulus energy into electrical energy, thus establishing a common signaling mechanism in all sensory systems" (Kandel, et all, 2000, Chapter 21, p. [415]). Electrical impulses are also refered to as action potentials or nerve impulses.

[5] The Oxford English Dictionary presents the following definition for cognition: „The mental action or process of acquiring knowledge and understanding through thought, experience, and the senses." Perception is its synonym: „The ability to see, hear, or become aware of something through the senses." According to this, I consider that the expressions 'object of perception' and the 'object of sensory cognition' can be used interchangeably.

or representative realist, or as someone who holds a representative theory of perception" (Crane, para 3.1.1).

Introducing sense-data as an intermediary between the mind and the world in the problem of perception is like introducing the concept of God in the problem of Genesis. It only complicates and transfers the problem. If God created the world, then how would one explain the creation of God? In an analogous manner, one could raise the question: How sense-data are created? How is the immediate (or direct) awareness, that is, the givenness of sense-data, explained? How are the private sense-data identical for each and every one of us, the proof of which is the consensus of subjects in the perception of the same reality, and what is the connection of such immediate experience with the independent reality which should provide us with the justification of beliefs about the physical world? Although the indirect realism admits the existence of the objective reality, it still does not offer any satisfying answers to these questions. Similar are the reasons why this theory is the target of criticism for the creation of a so-called 'veil of perception'[6] according to which sense-data compose the veil that covers the external world which in the end could lead to scepticism.

To claim that sense-data are simply given to us, that we are directly aware of them, without providing an explanation for the givenness is the same as claiming that God is the uncreated creator of the universe – dogmatically. This is why I consider the sense-data concept unnecessary addition to the naturalistic world picture.

The problem of the object of cognition in sense-data theories stems from and is related to the problematic conception of experience discussed above. Namely: "The sense-datum theory holds that when a person has a sensory experience, there is something of which they are aware. What the subject is aware of is the object of experience. The object of experience is that which is given to the senses, or the sense-datum..." (Crane, para. 3.1). The contents of the experience are the object of experience?

In addition, from what was set forth above, the experience is at the same time accepted as a source of knowledge both by empiricists and rationalists which creates additional confusion regarding the conception of experience.

It seems that it is the problematic conception of experience of the English empiricists discussed above that led to the birth of the sense-data

---

[6] See (Crane, para. 3.1.2).

theories of perception. As it was demonstrated, the experience presupposes knowledge; presence of sensations and perceptions in our consciousness already represents knowledge, knowledge of the most elementary particular things, and accordingly, these are not objects of cognition, since by definition an object is something that awaits to be recognized, something on which our power of cognition is focused. Sensations and perceptions can indisputably be objects of cognition, not sensory cognition, but other higher forms of cognition, such as cognition of universals, of which I will speak later.[7]

4. The electrical impulses are the most direct sensory material from which we obtain our complete knowledge of the outside world.[8] They are the only kind of material existence of the outside world that the material carrier of reason – the brain, is able to process and with that one can say that they are the most direct object of cognition. The existence and versatility of the outside world our senses code into variations of electrical impulses which are only suitable for processing by the reason. There is nothing in the reason that was previously not an electrical impulse, except reason itself, and everything we know of the outside world in a certain time existed only as information in an array of electrical impulses. This closer definition of the material provided by the senses will allow for a precise elaboration on the manner of its transformation in mental acts.

5. From the fact that reason creates things as we know them with the processing of electrical impulses it can be concluded that:

5.1. Things as we know them exist ontologically in our heads. A commonsense view, intuitive truth even, is the belief that things as we know them exist outside our heads and independently of our reason. This view is called naïve realism in philosophy, and it is rejected as wrong by cognitive sciences and serious philosophy, and even considered disgraceful by the majority of the philosophers.[9] We are taught to indiscriminately believe that things as we know them exist outside of us and independently of our reason, however, absurdly as it may sound, the reality is not like that. This conclusion stems directly from the fact that reason creates our knowledge through processing of electrical impulses. This processing

---

[7] Further on, with the analysis of higher forms of cognition, it will be demonstrated that the reason can be an object of cognition to itself, it can be self-aware.

[8] See *Principles of Neural Science* (Kandel, et all., 2000, chap. 21, p. 411-412) or especially the conclusion, page 428.

[9] See *Epistemological Problems of Perception* by Laurence BonJour (BonJour, para. 1, entry).

goes on in the brain, which is the material carrier of reason and accordingly, knowledge obtained as its result exists in our reason.

The book you are holding in your hands right now reflects light; the retina transforms the light into electrical impulses which through the optic nerve reach the visual cortex. We have the perception after the reason creates it by processing these electrical impulses in the visual cortex. This means that perception, the image of the book as we know it, is not outside us but in our head to the general dismay of naïve realists. The perception of its weight and hardness against our hands is also in our heads, since the book, as it is in the outside world, stimulates nerve endings in our hands which send an electrical signal to the touch and pressure center in our brains. There, in the brain, by processing the electrical impulse the sensation for weight and hardness is created. This thesis is nothing new in philosophy. "That this is so can be seen from the fact that all (or almost all) serious theories of perception agree that our perceptual experience *seems as if* it were awareness of a mind-independent world" (Crane, para. 2.1.1).

As a matter of fact, it can be said that modern epistemology begins with the awareness of this notion. This is very well noticed by the American philosopher Quincey who claims that "When Locke, followed by Hume and then Kant, showed that neither empiricism nor rationalism, nor both combined, could guarantee certain knowledge, that our minds could never know the world as it is in itself, philosophy retreated from the grand scheme of metaphysics, ontology, and cosmology, into epistemology" (Quincey, 149).

5.2. Things as we know them are of mental nature. If things are in our heads, then they must have mental nature because it is completely certain that real, material books, mountains, oceans, and other people do not exist there, only the ideas of these things. In this sense, everything we know is of mental nature. Bertrand Russell says that "...very many philosophers, perhaps most, have held that whatever is real must be in some sense mental, or at any rate that whatever we can know anything about must be in some sense mental. Such philosophers are called 'idealists'. Idealists tell us that what appears as matter is really something mental" (Russell, 1912, chap. III, conclusion).

The question of the nature of sensory experience, at least one of its aspects, in modern philosophy is known as 'problem of the external world', and it goes like this: "...what are the *immediate* objects of awareness in sensory experience or, in a variant but essentially equivalent terminology, of what is *given* in such experience" (BonJour, entry). Aside from naïve realism and its modern occurrence – direct realism, practically all other serious epistemological theories concur that what is given to us in the sensory experience are not material objects but entities of mental or other nature. This conclusion is derived from arguments such as hallucinations, illusions, perceptual relativity, scientific account of perception[10], and in other ways. Presentation and analysis of these arguments shall not be included in this text; they will merely be used as authority in support of the opinions expressed here.

5.3. Defining everything we know as mental does not mean we deny the existence of material objective reality. It is one thing to claim that there is an objective reality outside and independently of our reason and will, but it is something completely different to claim that this reality is identical to the reality as we know it. Based on conclusions reached above, the reality in general, meaning everything that exists, will be divided into two parts and the accepted terms for the respective parts shall be a reality in itself and reality as we know it. By *reality in itself* I mean the objective and material reality that exists outside and independently of our reason. This is a reality, as it is in itself, which is the object of cognition. By *reality, as we know it* I mean subjective and mental reality that exists inside and depends on our reason. This is the reality as we know it, which is created by processing reality in itself through the cognitive apparatus of man. As Werner Heisenberg puts it "...what we observe is not nature itself, but nature exposed to our method of questioning" (Heisenberg, 1958, 57). In Kantian terms reality as we know it is the reality of phenomena, and reality in itself is the reality of noumena.

****

Let us suppose that it is technically possible to set an electrode in the optic nerve of a certain subject which will perfectly capture the series of electrical impulses flowing through it while they, for example, observe Niagara Falls. If this recording through the same electrode is then played through the optic nerve of a subject which is located in London, then they will have the same visual experience and, in 'matrix' kind of reality,

---

[10] Nicely summed arguments supporting this thesis, which arise from illusion, perceptual relativity, hallucination, and the scientific account of perception are found in *Epistemological Problems of Perception* by Laurence BonJour (BonJour, para. 1.2).

will see the Niagara Falls in all their materiality and objectivity.[11] In any case, the thesis that all things we know as material and objective, as a matter of fact, exist in our heads and are of mental nature is no longer a specific philosophical position as it used to be in the past, but now, with the development of science it is a scientifically proven truth which, understood in all its depth, makes one's hair stand on end.

1.2 What is a thing?

Reality is a totality of things. Speaking in most general terms, our knowledge consists of things and our thinking examines the relations between different things, the origin of different things, the properties of things, or what is a certain thing. Previously it was discussed that things have a mental nature, that they exist in our heads, etc. However, seldom reach our thoughts so deep as to explicitly ask and analyze the question *what is a thing* in general. The entire system developed here begins and results from a possible answer to this utterly simple and fundamental, even if you please, childish question. Here is how Martin Heidegger asks it: "From the range of the basic questions of metaphysics we shall here ask this one question: "What is a thing?" The question is quite old. What remains ever new about it is merely that it must be asked again and again" (Heidegger, 1962, 1).

A thing is a determined being, and when we ask the question what a thing is, we actually search for the common in all determined beings. The scope of this generally understood term 'thing' is immense and boundless, and the differences between its individual members are countless. Probably the only property that can be acknowledged as common for all this enormous diversity is that things simply exist. When one thinks about them, no matter what they are like, without a doubt they exist in one way or the other, but this common property of theirs has little or no use value.

Still, they have something else in common. There is another uniting thread for all things, the discovery of which was the initial sparkle for this entire philosophy here before you. Namely: **all things are some kind of substantivized identity. Things are identities in themselves or identities**

---

[11] In an analogical manner, "Excitation of a particular sensory neuron, whether naturally or artificially by direct electrical stimulation, elicits the same sensation. For example, electrical stimulation of the auditory nerve can be used to signal tones of different frequencies in patients with deafness caused by damage to receptors in the inner ear" (Kandel, et all, 2000, Chapter 21, p. [416]).

between.[12] This is the thesis which I will try to prove in this chapter and which will be used as the basis for an alternative solution to the problem of knowledge.

For the needs of proving this thesis, we will divide things into two big groups: things that exist in space and/or in time and those that exist outside of space and outside of time. These are in fact particular and universal things, or universals, as they are also called. This categorization corresponds to the Aristotelian categorization of substance into first and second. First and foremost, particular things will be the subject of analysis here.

1.2.1 What is a particular thing?

Particular things are those that are in general given in sensory experiences, and according to this, we can call them sensible things. More precisely, these are sensations and perceptions, or colors, shapes, sounds, tactile properties of various sorts, material objects etc., understood as the content of the sensory experience. Particular things exist as segments from the space and/or time, and they belong to or constitute what we call objective reality. They can be named or not, however, we can point our finger to each particular thing and say – this!

If we define sensory experience in the simplest of ways, as a totality of things, then particular things would be parts of that reality. The question arises: what part of space or time exactly has the privilege to be oneness, to be perceived as one thing? Or, why exactly that part of the visual, auditory, and other sensory fields and exactly in those boundaries, has the privilege to be a thing?

Let us consider a random perceptual moment, the present – we are reading a book, that is, we are perceiving a piece of paper. By perceiving the piece of paper, we notice the black letters, the punctuation, and the white background. And the following question arises: why the entire white background of the paper is considered a thing, and the imaginary white triangle on the white paper in the upper right corner of the page is not? Why is the letter 'C' considered a thing, and not the third of the arch of the letter 'C' along with the little white part of the white surface above it? The question is only apparently trivial and banal, but as I am about to prove later, it is of crucial importance to understand the way in which we

---

[12] The meaning of these new terms will be elaborated further in the text. The expression 'identity in itself' will be used as the singular form of 'identities in themselves'. As a synonym for 'identity in itself' one can freely use the phrases 'uniformity in itself', 'unity in itself', 'sameness in itself', 'homogeneity in itself', etc.

know things. The answer is as follows: the letter 'C' is part of the space which is identical in itself or uniform in itself with its blackness, and the background is part of the space uniform in itself with its whiteness, and this is why these are considered things. On the other hand, it is rightful to argue that the mentioned hypothetical triangle is uniformity in itself with its white color, and still reason does not perceive it as a thing. The reason for this is because of uniformity, in this case, the whiteness, continues outside it, and the thing ends where uniformity ends. Beyond this boundary begins the different, the other thing. The triangle is not a thing because there is no possibility of its independence, a boundary which would separate it, and thus differentiate it from the remaining reality. In the second case, on the one side, there is no boundary, a difference that would separate one third from the rest of the letter, nor there is a boundary that would separate 'the little white surface' from the entire background. Also, there is no identity, a relation that would connect the part of the letter 'C' with the little white surface above it. Accordingly, the imaginary segment of the space is non-uniform in itself, that is, it is different in itself by color, partially black, partially white, and this is why it cannot exist as a thing. Put more plainly, these imaginary segments from the space are not identities in themselves, and therefore we do not know them as things.

Only uniform parts of the sensory experience can become objects of our thoughts, can be things. In this precise moment of perception, we can only think about, relate, or compare the letters, punctuation, and background. For example, it can be said that we like the design of the letters, that certain punctuation is misplaced, that the background is larger than the full stop, etc. On the other hand, the mentioned hypothetical non-uniformities cannot be objects of our thought, except only hypothetically, like in this example. We simply do not think about a third of the arch of the letter 'C' with the little white background above it, nor about the triangle because our reason does not recognize these imaginary spatial segments as things.

Further, in addition to these, so to say, two-dimensional things, the three-dimensional material objects are also things. A thing is a book itself which is a part of the space that is identical in itself with its materiality opposed to the empty space around it. In general, each three-dimensional object around us is that part of space which is uniform in itself in its ability to reflect or emit light or in any other property that determines its materiality. Countless things are included and shown as uniformities through this generalization.

All this can be confirmed with a thought-provoking exercise: look around you, in your immediate surroundings. Point at things around you: objects, parts of objects, parts of parts, two-dimensional surfaces of objects, shadows, the empty space between them, and in general, everything that can be called a thing, and you will notice that they are all identities in themselves by color or by some other property. Stars are uniformities in themselves by their shine as opposed to the dark skies around them, and the skies around them are uniformities in themselves by their darkness, and this is why they are known as things. Try also to count sounds that you hear in a certain time interval, and you will notice that each counted sound is a time segment uniform in itself and if pitch, intensity, or tone changes, then we are talking about a different sound, that is, about a different thing. In fact, we count as many things, in this case, sounds, as there are uniformities. Same applies to smells, tastes, and all another sensory, i.e. particular things.

There are specific particular things that due to the vastness of the uniform spatial or temporal segment that defines them, are not given to us directly or completely in the sensory experience. Regardless, these are also uniformities in themselves. These are a couple of examples: a day as a temporal segment is a thing since it is uniform in the presence of sunlight, visibility, the presence of sun in the perceptual field. The Middle Ages as a time interval is a thing since it is uniform in itself by the ruling of the church as a property. The river Nile is a thing since it is a uniform spatial segment, simply because of the water with all its properties as opposed to the desert surrounding it. The city of Skopje is a thing since it is a uniform spatial segment of the buildings as opposed to the natural setting around it. If the boundaries separating uniformities are blurred, or the transition from one uniformity to another is gradual, it only means things are vaguely defined, and nothing more.

It can be concluded that the most fundamental property of things which are spatial and/or temporal sequences is the fact that they are all a kind of substantivized identity in themselves, a non-difference in themselves according to one or more properties. Identity in itself is what a certain spatial or temporal segment defines as oneness, as a thing.

1.2.2 What is a universal thing?

Universals are unities of particular or less general things. For example, the universal 'human' is a unity of the less general things 'men' and 'women'. The universal 'men' is a unity of all individuals such as Socrates, Heraclitus, etc. However, this unity is not arbitrary but founded on identity. Namely, each universal does not unite random things, but those with one or more common, that is identical properties. This understanding is widely accepted in philosophy. Bertrand Russell confirms this by saying "...a *universal* will be anything which may be shared by many particulars..." (Russell, 1912, chap. IX). Since it is shared by them it is something they have in common, and a thing in common is, of course, what is same, i.e. identical between particularities. For example, the universal 'man' is a unity of all particular living beings which are identical according to the properties of having a reason, upright gait, the ability to laugh, etc. The universal 'metal' is a unity of all particular materials which are identical according to the properties of meltability and forgeability.

From this, it can be concluded that the universals are substantivized identities between the particular things or less general things. They are not simple identities in themselves as particular things are, but complex unities of the multeity or unities of varieties. In contrast to the particular things, it can be said that these are identities between.

****

Unbelievably similar thoughts on the nature of things can be found in Plotinus. Here is how he begins the ninth tractate from his sixth Ennead:

> It is in virtue of unity that beings are beings.
> This is equally true of things whose existence is primal and of all that are in any degree to be numbered among beings. What could exist at all except as one thing? Deprived of unity, a thing ceases to be what it is called: no army unless as a unity: a chorus, a flock, must be one thing. Even house and ship demand unity, one house, one ship; unity gone, neither remains thus even continuous magnitudes could not exist without an inherent unity; break them apart and their very being is altered in the measure of the breach of unity.
> Take plant and animal; the material form stands a unity; fallen from that into a litter of fragments, the things have lost their being; what was is no longer there; it is replaced by quite other things — as many others, precisely, as possess unity. (Plotinus, Ninth Tractate, §1)

Then he continues: "Anything that can be described as unity is so in the precise degree in which it holds a characteristic being; the less or more the degree of the being, the less or more the unity" (Ibid.). There is a striking overlap with the philosophy presented here. Plotinus uses the term 'unity' where I use 'uniformity' or 'identity', and the meaning of these terms is exactly the same. He even at one moment uses the phrase 'inherent unity' where 'inherent' has the same meaning as 'in itself'. These lines can be integrated into the philosophy presented here without any changes.

I came across similar thoughts in Heidegger whose philosophy is inspired by Plotinus. Speaking of the principle of identity in his work, *Identity and Difference*, Heidegger points out that identity is primarily a principle of the being, and then the highest principle of thought: "The principle of identity speaks of the Being of beings. As a law of thought, the principle is valid only insofar as it is a principle of Being that reads: "To every being as such there belongs identity, the unity with itself" (Heidegger, 1957, 26). Then he continues: "What the principle of identity, heard in its fundamental key, states is exactly what the whole of Western European thinking has in mind – and that is: **the unity of identity forms a basic characteristic in the Being of beings** (Emphasis Mine)" (Ibid.). This thought of his is a vivid reminder of the view presented here that the basic characteristic common for each particular thing is the identity in itself and that each thing is a substantivized identity. Heidegger develops this idea further in another direction, investigating the relation of man and being while this work is directed toward the problem of cognition.

Finally, it can be summarized that particular and universal things are substantivized identities. Particular things are identities in themselves, and universal things are identities between. Everything we know as a thing is a substantivized identity, and everything that is identity is a thing or has the potential to become a thing. Identity is the fundamental property of things, long forgotten truth since the childhood of reason, forgotten because it is so obvious and banal it seems unworthy of attention. However, the extraordinary importance of this realization regarding the theory of knowledge is yet to be proven after it is related to the previously established fact that things, as we know them, are in fact mental entities.

1.3 Knowledge of sensations – where the material touches the mental

The scene is set, and now the attention can be directed to one of the most important open questions in theory of knowledge and philosophy in general: turning material provided by the senses into sensations, i.e. into acts of cognitive awareness. The key question in the theory of knowledge is what happens to the material, electrical impulses after they reach the brain? In which way are they processed by the reason to obtain from them mental things, of course, sensations and perceptions first? This is maybe one of the greatest mysteries in philosophy, and I would note that there has not been a satisfactory solution to this perennial problem so far. In this chapter, an attempt will be made at a probable explanation on the transition from the material to mental, as well as on the relation between the objective and real world of things in themselves and our subjective cognitive picture of it – the reality as we know it.

The realization that all particular things are identities in themselves, although apparently trivial, is of invaluable importance for it enables us to understand the relation between material provided by the senses and things which the reason creates from it through the process of cognition. The problem of the genesis of things as we know them is, in fact, a problem of cognition. As we well know, each creator leaves a seal on their creation and, accordingly, each creation tells us something of its creator. In this case, the seal is the identity in itself that the reason gives as a common property of all things it creates, and exactly this fact will allow us to answer the questions how are things created and what is the nature of reason, accordingly. Electrical impulses are the leading player of the objective material reality in itself, and sensations, are the leading player of the subjective mental reality as we know it; the answer is hidden in their cognitive rendezvous. Both realities meet here. The relation between the mental and the material, that is, between the nature of our ideas and the nature of electrical impulses is the easiest to notice when analyzing sensations. These are the simplest mental things, and they are in the most direct relation to the physical from which they are created.

Let us make a thought-provoking experiment on the cognitive process of reality in real time. We are in a dark room. Before us is a screen which in certain time intervals lights up in different colors. The color changes five times: for the first three seconds the screen is red, the next five seconds it is blue, and then for one second it is yellow, etc., as shown in the figure below. In the concrete real temporal segment when we recognize the red color our vision is reached by light at a frequency of 400 Hz; when we recognize blue, the light frequency is slightly above 600 Hz, etc. respectively, as shown in the first graph of the figure.

Furthermore, the eye transforms this light into electrical impulses. The coding of the property of frequency of the light is a complex and still insufficiently known process.[13] The properties of these impulses are

---

[13] This is a complex problem that is the focus of numerous sciences, mostly neuroscience, cognitive psychology (or cognitive science), and philosophy of perception. For more see *Principles of Neural Science* (Kandel, et all., 2000, chap. 29, Color Vision).

unknown to us,[14] but what is certain is that for each stimulation of the retina by light with certain properties we obtain an output with certain properties; when light changes, the impulse changes, and when light is uniform, then the impulse is uniform, and therefore every time that we will have a uniform input, we will have a uniform output as it is shown in the second graph where the unknown property of the impulse is marked with 'x'. If this would not be the case, then with each glance at the same objective reality we would obtain a different random image from our reason which would disable our practical functioning.

Electrical impulses generated thus reach the brain through the optic nerve where their processing by the reason begins. These impulses are the material provided by the senses from which the reason creates the five mental things, that is, in this case, the five sensations (colors) which are uniformities in themselves as it is shown in the last graph. This is the point where reality in itself becomes a reality as we know it.

---

[14] It is much simpler, for example, to code the property of intensity, not only of light but also, generally, of all other sensory stimuli: "Stimulus intensity is encoded by the frequency of action potentials in sensory nerves" (Kandel, et. all, 2000, chap. 21, p. [422]). Quite simple is the coding of the temporal property: "The quantitative features of sensory stimuli measured in psychophysical studies are signaled by the firing patterns of the activated population of sensory neurons. The details of neuronal activity-how long a neuron fires, how fast, and how many neurons firing-encode the intensity and time course of sensory experience" (Kandel, et. all, 2000, chap. 21, p. [422]). Or, considering auditory perception: "The acoustic sensitivity of the axons in the cochlear nerve mirrors the innervation pattern of the spiral ganglion cells" (Kandel, et. al, 2000, chap. 30, p. [602]).

Reason as a cognitive subject 17

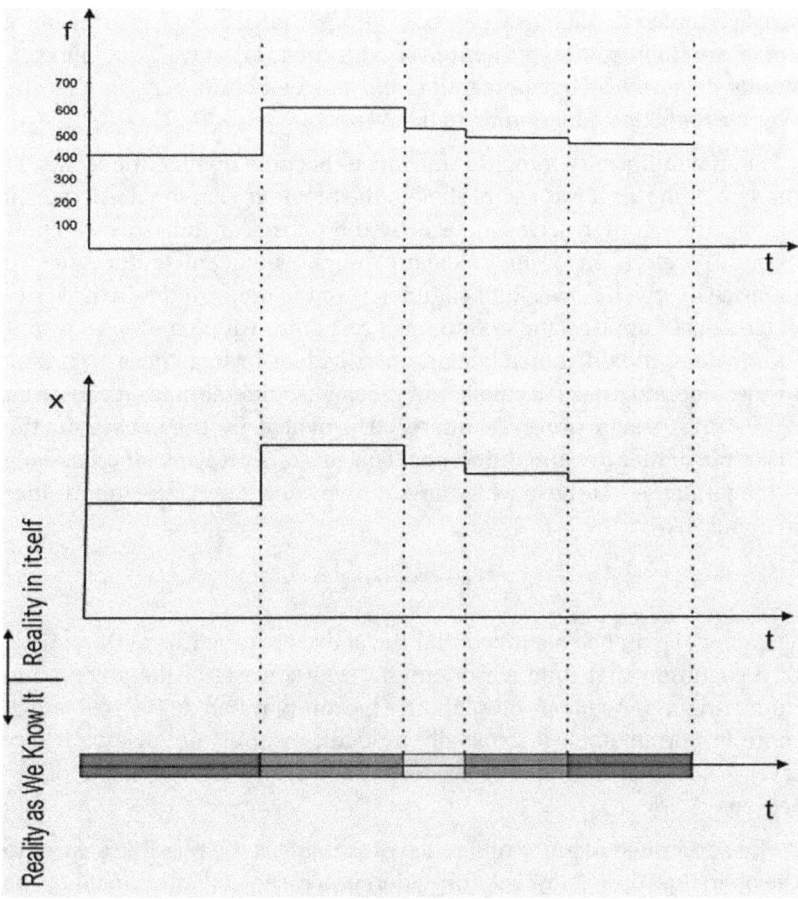

(Figure, Triple graph)

1.3.1 Heartcore

This analysis points to a fundamental conclusion. We notice that in this close encounter between the mental and physical reality, uniformities in the material provided by the senses in real time correspond completely to the uniformities in mental reality. "Although our perceptions of the size, shape, and color of objects are derived entirely from patterns of light that strike our retinas, our perceptions nevertheless appear to correspond to the physical properties of objects. In most instances, we can use our perceptions to manipulate an object and to predict aspects of its behavior. Perception, we can show, organizes an object's essential properties well enough to let us handle the object appropriately" (Kandel et al., 2000, chap. 21, p. [412]). If we perceive uniformity in a non-uniform sensory material, then we perceive things that do not exist, because things are uniformities in themselves. This means that we would be constantly deceived by our perception and not be able to rely on it in the everyday practical functioning in the world.

Material uniformity somehow mirrors to become mental uniformity. At the same time, as it was established in the previous chapter, these mental uniformities in themselves are exactly the particular things as we know them. Therefore, in order to create things which are uniformities in themselves which correspond completely to the uniformities in the series of electrical impulses, the reason must recognize where the series is uniform, where the difference begins, and divide it in sequences according to these boundaries. It actually identifies and differentiates, or in other words: **the reason processes material provided by the senses on the principle of identity and difference.** This reason's principle of processing is the fundamental cause why things, as we know them, are uniformities in themselves.

****

Therefore, it can be concluded that the active creating role of the subject of a cognition that rationalists emphasized consists of identifying and differentiating. As it can be seen, the reason plays an active role, much more important than it is usually thought, even at the lowest sensory level because even the simplest sensations are in fact creations of the reason.

Thus described identity-difference processing is the possible answer to the open question – How is information processed and interpreted by the brain? This transformation of the material into mental is what is unjustifiably overlooked in sense-datum epistemological theories by simply presenting sensations as given or as such we are directly aware of without understanding that the key problem of cognition is the explanation of the act of givenness itself.

Similar thought-provoking experiments such as these can also be done for the perception in space where the variable 'space from where the light comes' is coded in a place in the retina where the impulse is being generated. Uniform temporal segments when the ear receives uniform sound waves become things as we know them that is, sounds, in auditory perception. The same goes for all remaining senses: "The modern study of sensation began in the nineteenth century with the pioneering work of Weber and Fechner in sensory psychophysics. They discovered that despite the diversity of sensations we experience, all sensory systems convey four basic types of information when stimulated—modality, location, intensity, and timing. Together, these four elementary attributes of a stimulus yield sensation. The fact that all sensory systems convey the same type of information may be one reason why they have such similar organization" (Kandel et al., 2000, chap. 21, p. [413]).

This identification and differentiation is obviously happening very fast considering the multiety of sensations we are capable of recognizing in one single moment. This happens without us being conscious of it and outside of the control of our will, automatically. Our knowledge of ourselves, our self-awareness never go as deep as to be aware of this process.

Some interesting consequences that stem from the thusly established principle of processing the material provided by the senses that clarify the relation between reality in itself and reality as we know it, and cast new light on certain ontological and epistemological problems, will be presented further.

1.3.2 On the difference between being and non-being

One of these problems is the problem of non-being. We undoubtedly possess knowledge of the non-being, it is present in our consciousness, we think about it, we have a name for it. Since it is the object of our thoughts, undoubtedly the non-being exists, which is a scandalous and paradoxical conclusion. Let us set this problem in a different, more precise way. With the cases presented so far it was established that the reason creates things by processing material provided by the senses, but only those things we know as beings. What we failed to go into, and which is of crucial importance, is the profound difference that the reason makes between being and non-being. This is actually the difference which is created at the reception, that is, non-reception of the sensory signals. It is a disturbing fact that aside from the ideas of beings, the reason knows also of non-beings, although in the moment of their perception the senses do not provide material of any kind. For example, from the empty space or darkness, light is neither emitted nor reflected. How is it then possible that we have the idea of the empty space or the darkness, how do we recognize them as things then? Or, how does the reason create an idea of silence when at the moment it perceives it, the ear does not provide it with any kind of material? Is this fact contradictory to the view that the complete knowledge comes from our senses and does in this case knowledge transcend experience?

The answer comes from the fact which was established earlier, that things, as we know them, are uniformities in themselves. Namely, silence and darkness and all other non-beings[15] are uniform segments of the space and/or time, and this is due to the absence of sensory stimuli. It is certain that the reason actively identifies and differentiates both when it receives sensory stimuli and when it does not, and for it, the spatial or the temporal segment when it does not receive any stimuli is a uniformity same as all other uniformities. It, accordingly, creates things from these uniformities, i.e. it creates the non-beings. Now uniformities in themselves can be ontologically divided into two general types – beings and non-beings. The non-beings do not exist in reality in itself but only in the reality as we know it. This would be the answer to the ontological paradox from above.

This is a striking illustration of the difference between reality as we know it and reality in itself which leads us to the conclusion that the reason does not recognize as a thing what really exits, as the 'common sense' tells us, but only what is a certain uniformity in itself. Beings and non-beings exist side by side in reality as we know it and according to this one can conclude that we do not know what really exists, but we know the identity-difference structure of objective reality. In this sense, reality as we know it is a broader term than reality in itself since we have ideas for things that do not exist in reality in itself, and these are, above all, ideas of non-beings. At the same time, exactly the presence of sensory stimuli allows for one to become aware of their absence since only the presence enables one to become aware of the absence. In this respect, one should bear in mind that, if non-beings do not exist in the reality as we know it, then beings as ideas will not exist either according to the dialectical law of the battle of the opposites. Both subjects of the relation of difference always exist only in relation to each other, they never exist separately, so the being is known only in relation to the non-being and vice versa. The being gives sense to the non-being and vice versa, one exists only in relation to the other and only as different than the other, and if one disappears, the other will disappear too. What would light be without darkness and what would the sound be without silence? What use would we have to the term light if there was no darkness? What would it denote and what would we use it for? In a similar way the universal 'being' is derived only because of this possibility of awareness of non-

---

[15] From the aspect of the entire perception field which fuels the reason, subtypes of differences between 'being' and 'non-being' can be distinguished according to our sensory organs. These would be: light – dark, sound – silence, touch - non-touch, smell – non-smell, warm – cold. Terms of non-beings for which there is no suitable word in the English language are freely derived with a simple negation of the term used for the beings.

beings. Generally, the being can be known as existent only in its relation to the difference to the non-being as non-existent.

1.3.3 On the quantitative relation between reality as we know it and reality in itself

From the thought-provoking experiment analyzed above, it could be concluded that each specific sensation originates from a specific segment of the material provided by the senses. At the same time, the number of sensible things originating from certain material provided by the senses does not depend on its quantity, only on its quality, that is, its diverseness in itself. If the screen in the previously mentioned thought-provoking experiment emits light only with one frequency – of the same duration, from the same quantity of material provided by the senses, the reason will create only one thing. Similarly, if one observes the clear blue skies for one hour, one would get an enormous quantity of light, and still, from this enormous quantity of material provided by the senses, the reason will create only one thing.

Generally speaking, the quantity of existence of reality in itself is a non-changeable category. The principle of conservation of energy applies to the reality in itself, which points to the fact that energy cannot be created nor destroyed – it only changes its shape. On the other hand, the quantity, i.e. the number of things in reality as we know it depends on the quantity of uniformity in reality in itself (of course, those that can be coded by light and other media). This means that reality as we know it can be created and destroyed depending on the change of identity-difference structure of reality in itself.

For reality in itself, it is completely irrelevant in which way it exists, in how many parts, in what shapes. Nature is completely indifferent toward us. Following this logic until its end, if in one imaginary state the objective reality reaches an absolute uniformity, without differences in itself, then through the process of its cognition we will obtain a completely uniform impulse. From this impulse the reason will not be able to separate uniform segments because there are no boundaries, there are no differences based on which it can establish the boundaries. This, in the end, means that the reason will not be able to create things as we know them, that is, that reality as we know it will not exist. And the other way around: at the other end of the spectrum, if the objective reality finds itself in a state of absolute diversity in itself, absolute chaos, where our cognitive apparatus would not be able to locate at least one separate uniform spatial or temporal segment, then again reality as we know it will not exist. Since it is certain that the reason possesses a certain 'threshold of sensibility' this means that if uniformities are too minuscule spatially or temporally, the reason would not be able to know them. To illustrate this, we could use the occurrence of intensifying frequency of beats – at one moment we will start recognizing a uniform sound. This is how increasing diversity at a certain moment transforms into its contrast and becomes complete uniformity.

Absolute uniformity of everything means naught. Reality to a man that lives in a completely white room without windows and drinking only milk would be practically zero. In a similar way, an absolute difference of everything means naught, destruction of reality as we know it. The existence of our spirits, of our reason, is completely preconditioned and proportional to the existence of diversity and uniformities in the world through a dialectical play where their existence is mutually conditioned according to the law of battle and unity of the opposites.

To sum up, being to us is uniformity in itself, and being in itself is matter.[16] In both considered extremes, the quantity of existence of reality in itself remains unchanged while reality as we know it ceases to exist. This confirms the fact that objective material existence is not enough per se and deciding for the existence of reality as we know it, but that matter is just a precondition for the existence of uniformities in themselves, which in turn are a precondition for the existence of things in reality as we know it. The possibility of reality as we know it to be created and destroyed as opposed to the destructiveness of reality in itself is another argument in support of the difference between the two realities.

1.3.4 Problem of justification

From these new notions also results the possibility to cast a light on one aspect of the so-called 'problem of the external world' related to the way in which our beliefs for the external material world, that is, the reality in itself, can be justified on the basis of sensory experience.

We know that the Kantian reality in itself, although being an undisputed ontological reality, remained gnoseologically irrelevant, an outcome that may result in agnosticism and subjective idealism. However, despite this, I consider the gap between reality as we know it and reality in itself not to be irreconcilable. Next I will present the penetration of reality in itself into the reality as we know it, the direct relation between these two realities from which arises the gnoseological relevance of reality in itself: the sensory experience as we know it is a totality of things which are

---

[16] In this instance 'in itself' has a different meaning, i.e. 'uniformity in itself' refers to internal identity, while 'being in itself (reality in itself)' refers to reality as it is, unprocessed by the cognitive apparatus of man, the transcendent realm of the noumenon.

uniformities in themselves and correspond exactly to the uniform segments of electrical impulses. In turn, uniform segments of the impulses are induced by the senses when they are stimulated by uniform media such as light, sound, etc. In turn, media are uniform when they are emitted or reflected from uniform objective reality. From this causal sequence, as it was seen earlier, it can be concluded that things as we know them correspond completely to the uniformities in objective reality which is the object of cognition. In this sense, one can argue that both realities, although completely different in nature, have the identical identity-difference structure. Where identities or differences exist in reality in itself, they exist in the reality as we know it, and this is precisely what allows us to function practically in reality in itself. Our reality is a kind of identity-difference model of objective reality, only the differences and the identities, here and there, are between completely different actors, one of objective material nature, and the other of mental, spiritual nature. Objectivity of our knowledge as a property, the identity between nature and spirit, being and thinking, and the justification of our beliefs of the external world results from this order of the transformation of reality in itself into reality as we know it. Or, as Spinoza brilliantly put it: "The order and connection of ideas is the same as the order and connection of things" (Spinoza, 1677, 119).

****

This is, however, an idealized representation of the relation between these two realities. In the real cognitive process, a big group of questions arises related to the authenticity, that is the quality of each of these, so called, transformations or information codings. A more thorough analysis of these would call for copious work including separate analysis of each sense. It would mean straying from the topic at hand which is the functioning of the human reason. Therefore, I shall try to briefly locate and sketch only a part of these imperfections, and I will mainly comment on the sense of sight.

First and foremost, as it is well known from the material reality in itself, only certain types of matter, that is, energy is known most directly and authentically. Our senses are able to receive only a certain small number of objective material existence types, and these are electromagnetic radiation in a certain specter which we know as light, mechanical waves which we know as sound, certain volatile chemical substances by the smell, and certain chemical substances by the taste. The remaining greater part of the objective existence, above all, material objects, we know indirectly, mainly with the help of light.

1. Imperfections in cognition are mostly related to the first transformation, and this is the coding of material reality into the light. How authentically is the light with its abilities of variation able to express the abilities of variation of matter? Light possesses only four properties according to which it varies: frequency, intensity, space from where it is emitted or reflected, and time in which it is emitted or reflected. The stream of light which stimulates our sense of sight is a structure of these properties. In turn, the matter is much more complex and possesses a much larger number of properties. What is certain is that light can transmit information on the existence or the non-existence of a material object in a certain time, wherein the existence of matter will be coded in existence of light in that exact time, and vice versa. Then, it is certain that it can transmit information on the shape, size, and position of the material object in space – properties which will be coded in shape, size, and position in the part of the retina where the light falls and which induces impulses. Or, to be more precise, it is certain that light transmits quality information on the spatial-temporal identity-difference structure in the objective reality.

However, the coding of the numerous remaining properties of matter in properties of light is far more disputable. It is clear that we have to accept that we cannot claim any idealized perfect knowledge of reality in itself which would mean a complete identity, in every sense of reality as we know it and reality in itself, because it is simply impossible the world as is in itself to be located in our heads. So, although the type of light which is reflected is not the essential reflection of the matter, in a certain sense, for our cognition needs it would be enough when the different matter would reflect different light. It is, however, certain, that there are different material substances that reflect light with an identical frequency or identical substances that reflect a different frequency which results in an imperfection in cognition which can be corrected with the combination of knowledge provided from other senses, as well as with using knowledge gained through experience.

Additionally, we cannot say that uniformities in themselves according to color and intensity always mirror the essential uniformities of the matter. Through frequency, that is, color, for example, light can transmit to us the information on the nature of the surface of a certain material object, but only that two surfaces are identical or different. The essence of their differences is not expressed with the difference between two colors. For example, the meaning of the difference between gold and papers is not expressed in the difference between white and yellow. Only through experience, on the basis of cases from the past, we know the meaning of colors, that is, which color is a code of what or which properties of the matter. Through experience, we learn that the green color of the plant means that the plant is alive, as opposed to the dark color which means that the plant is dead. Generally, it can be said that except existence and 'spatial and temporal' properties of matter, the codes of other properties are indirect, so they are known indirectly or in combination with other senses.

This conclusion takes us to John Locke who offers the most explicit elaboration of the distinction between primary and secondary properties. Locke thought that real material objects possess only primary properties in which he also included solidity, extension, figure, motion or rest, and number, and not secondary properties such as color, sounds, taste, and felt temperature. He considered the second subjective results of the perception which exist only in our heads (Locke, 1689, book II, chap. 8). It can be noticed that Locke's primary properties mainly correspond to the 'spatial-temporal' properties analyzed above. However, unlike Locke, my opinion is that even primary properties as we know them are of mental nature. They are only directly, and with it, best-coded properties of the objective reality in the sense that existence of matter is coded into existence of light; while size and shape are coded into size and shape of the light imprint in the retina.

Knowledge results from the senses and in order for us to know any property of the external world we must reduce it to a sense expression. The larger part of experimental science and technology deals exactly with this reduction. The clock is a device for reduction of the sensory unperceivable time to a perceivable sensory position of its hands. Particle detectors are devices for reduction of the sensory unperceivable microparticles to perceivable sensory traces in the chamber, and litmus paper reduces the sensory unperceivable chemical composition of matter to a sensory perceivable color of the paper. The question is, whether there are properties that cannot be reduced to a sensory expression, i.e. are there properties that remain incognizable?

It can be concluded that the first type of imperfections of cognition results from the limited abilities of light and other media to code every property of matter. Uniformities in the material reality are not perfectly mirrored in uniformities according to the properties of light. Best mirrored properties of matter are existence/non-existence, as well as 'spatial-temporal' properties.

2. Another type of imperfections in cognition results from the second transformation that is the transformation of light, sound, and other media in electrical impulses. This gives rise to the question – With what degree of authenticity can our sensory organs code uniformities of media

into uniformities of impulses? This is something that neurophysiologists need to answer.

3. The third transformation relates to the coding of uniformities of the stream of impulses into things as we know them. First arises a technical question – With what degree of authenticity is the reason capable of recognizing uniformities in impulses? Additionally, the specific manner of processing of the material provided by the senses is definitely that which makes the difference between the two realities. Reality as we know it is a reality in itself processed on the principle of identity and difference. Instead of claiming that the reason cognizes reality, maybe it is more accurate to claim that the reason builds it, creates it. It is, however, disputable whether we can at all talk about things in reality in itself when we know that things are created by our reason. It is questionable whether the understanding of uniformity as a thing is the correct or the best way of cognition of such given reality in itself? Who knows what reality as we know it would be like if our reason functioned on some other principles. *"Rational thought is interpretation according to a scheme that we cannot throw off"* (Nietzsche, 1901, note 522, 283).

****

It is clear that the physical reality and the mental image of it do not have the same ontological status and are of different nature, but on the other hand, one can claim that, to a certain extent, they represent synchronized identity-difference structures. It seems that all imperfections of knowledge are related to a lack of differences which are lost between codings, however, if there already is a difference in the reality as we know it, then it is certain that this difference exists in reality in itself. Considering this, it seems that the identity-difference structure of reality as we know it is more incomplete than the identity-difference structure of reality in itself.

Analogously, as sounds of music and electromagnetic particles on the magnetic tape on which the music is recorded are of completely different nature, but they have identical identity-difference structure and when the tape is reproduced its uniform segments become uniform segments in music. This is where both worlds, both realities, come into contact: reality as we know it and reality in itself, this "…wonderful correlation between the *phenomenon of knowledge* and the *object of knowledge*…" (Husserl, 1907, 68) of which Husserl speaks. The (imperfect) identity of the identity-difference structures is the reason that enables justification in our beliefs created on the basis of the sensory experience of reality in itself.

1.4 Cognition of perceptions

Perception follows sensation. In this chapter, an attempt will be made to demonstrate that perceptions, same as sensations, are known on the principle of identity and difference by using the previous analysis of cognition of sensations, as well as the analysis of principles of the Gestalt theory. The main focus will be on the visual and audio perceptions.

First, let us suggest a criterion for distinction between sensations and perceptions. We need an analysis of the modes of differentiation of material provided by the senses to achieve this. As it was already mentioned before, there are several modes of differentiation according to which the reason can separate the stream of material provided by the senses. First of all, the reason divides on the basis of the following: existence or non-existence of the impulse – subject which was touched upon in the chapter about the difference between being and non-being. Let us call this an ontological mode of differentiation, common to all senses, and because of it, we obtain segments from time and space which are uniformities in themselves according to the existence or the non-existence of the impulse in the stream of material provided by the senses. The complications with further analysis of modes result from our incomplete knowledge of the nature and structure of electrical impulses. This is why I will simply skip this and draw a parallel between modes of differentiation of visual and audio sensations as we know them and modes of differentiation of light and sound. I consider this 'skip' a right decision under the assumption that the modes of light and sound differentiation mirror and are equivalent to the modes of differentiation of impulses which in their turn mirror and are equivalent to the modes of differentiation of sensations.

Let us see which they are: visual sensory things as we know them can be differentiated according to color and brightness which is equivalent to the modes of light – frequency and intensity. Auditory sensory things, the sounds, can be differentiated according to the pitch and loudness which is equivalent to the modes of differentiation of the sound waves according to frequency and intensity. However, these listed are by no means the only modes of differentiation. I presume that these are the basic modes which form the basis for the formation of other more complex modes of differentiation. The sound, for example, can be differentiated according to the timbre which is essentially a combination of sound wave frequencies. Contrast is determined by the difference in the color and brightness, etc. Further, it will be shown that movement, size, orientation, shape, etc., are also considered modes.[17]

According to this analysis, an attempt will be made to define sensations and make a clear distinction between sensations and perceptions: spatial or temporal segments as we know them, which are uniform in themselves according to all the modes of differentiation, I here call sensations. A visual sensation to me is a unique segment of the visual-spatial field of uniform color and uniform brightness or uniform darkness while the auditory sensation would be a unique interval filled with uniform pitch and intensity of the sound or with uniform silence. Thusly defined, sensations are the most basic products of cognition. They are indivisible, that is, cannot be analyzed by the reason. They are, I would dare say, logical atoms, basic building blocks of knowledge.

Perceptions, as opposed to sensations, are complex things composed of two or more sensations which are uniform in themselves at least according to one mode of differentiation. Further the manner of creation of these complex uniformities in themselves will be reflected upon, and in the beginning, a distinction will be made between two types of perceptions: the first type are the perceptions that exist in one and only one segment of space and/or time. Perceptions of the second type exist in more segments of space and/and time. The first type will be considered in the pages to follow.

From the multiple opportunities for differentiating the stream of sensory signals arise the opportunities for the existence of complex uniformities in themselves as they are, for example, material objects. They are singled out as uniformities in themselves according to their property to reflect light as opposed to the empty space around them. However, although they are uniform in themselves according to this ontological mode, they can reflect light with different colors from different parts of theirs, and so they can be a complex uniformity in themselves; or, if a group of successive sounds with different pitches can have the same intensity, and so the complex group will represent a complex uniformity in itself according to intensity. These perceptions are particular things just like sensations because they exist in one and only one segment of space or time. They are different from sensations because they can be analyzed, divided by the reason into elementary sensations which they are composed of and which to them, in this case, are properties.

---

[17] How are more complex modes formed from the basic, if we can at all talk about basic modes, as well as the question of the mode–thing relation, remain open. This is in fact the old metaphysical question of nature and the origin of properties.

There is a lot more to learn about the manners of grouping sensations into second type perceptions from the Gestalt theory.[18] "Kant's concept of a priori knowledge left its mark on Gestalt psychology, which holds that aspects of perception are the product of the brain's inborn capacity to order simple sensations in characteristic ways" (Kandel et al., 2000, chap. 21, p. [412]). This inborn capacity to order simple sensations in characteristic ways is one of the faces of reason. Gestalt theory mainly analyzes the visual perception and strives to determine the principles based on which the visual perceptional field is organized in units (perceptions), i.e. things, separate from the rest of the visual field. I can say that the principles of this theory are greatly confirming the thesis in this chapter that perceptions are formed on the principle of identity and difference. There is no definitive list of these principles, so I present here the most discussed and most generally accepted according to Todorovic:[19]

1. "The common fate principle states that elements tend to be perceived as grouped together if they move together" (Todorovic, 2008). If they move together this means that they are identical by their property of movement, hence, this principle actually claims a unification of elements according to identity.

2. "The similarity principle claims that elements tend to be integrated into groups if they are similar to each other" (ibid.). This principle is the most direct confirmation of the thesis in this work. The similarity is essentially partial identity, which means identity according to one or more properties, and according to this, this principle claims grouping of ele-

---

[18] They deal little or not at all with the formation of sensations. They come closest to exploring sensations with the so-called types of organization of the visual field that in the Gestalt theory is known as the 'figure-ground articulation'. The example from the first chapter (1.2.1), with the letters and the background is actually an illustration of this type of organization of the visual field. Gestalt theorists argue that the visual field can be divided into elementary dots (pixels) that could theoretically be combined into units of different ways. Thus they conclude that of all possible options for combining them, reason often opts for only one combination that it will recognize as perception. This property of reason is called 'fundamental aspect of field organization'. But they do not arrive at an answer to the question – Why is that combination so special as to become a perception. The answer, as we saw earlier, is that this combination is special because it is the only one forming uniformities in themselves.

[19] Principles here are very scarcely articulated. I recommend (Todorovic, 2008) where they are explained in more detail and illustrated with simple drawings that largely simplify their understanding.

ments which are identical according to one property, for example, light, color, size, orientation, or shape.

3. "The continuity principle: oriented units or groups tend to be integrated into perceptional wholes if they are aligned with each other" (ibid.). This principle, in fact, claims unification of sensations or simple perceptions which are identical according to the property of lying on the same line.

4. "The closure principle: elements tend to be grouped together if they are parts of a closed figure" (ibid.). This principle actually claims unification of sensations or simple perceptions which are identical according to the property of belonging to a figure.

5. "The past experience principle: elements tend to be grouped together if they were together often in the past experience of the observer" (ibid.). If elements appeared together in the past experiences of the observer, then they are identical according to the property of belonging to those experiences. According to this, this principle also claims unification according to identity.

6. "The symmetry principle (symmetrical components will tend to group together)" (ibid.). Symmetry is actually a relation of identity according to shape and size between two halves, meaning the grouping of two symmetrical components in a whole is grouping according to identity.

7. "The proximity principle: elements tend to be perceived as aggregated into groups if they are near each other" (ibid.). Strictly speaking, elements are not in the same space, and no two things can ever be in the same space. Closeness is a relative category and only things whose distance is relatively smaller in comparison to the distance between them, and the other surrounding elements are considered close. However, due to certain, not entirely clear causes,[20] the reason experiences relatively close things as being in the same space, in the same time, and according to this, it can be said that this principle actually claims unification of sensations or simple perceptions which are identical according to the space they belong to.

8. "The common region principle: elements tend to be grouped together if they are located within the same closed region" (ibid.). Or, the identity between elements according to their belonging to the same closed region.

9. "The good Gestalt principle: elements tend to be grouped together if they are parts of a pattern which is a good Gestalt, meaning as simple,

---

[20] We will look into this problem again later, in chapter 2.5 *Association*.

orderly, balanced, unified, coherent, regular, etc. as possible, given the input" (ibid.) The formulation of this principle is complex and vague, so it cannot be directly said what identity comprised of is. However, I will use Todorovic's note to elaborate further: "It has been suggested that most Gestalt principles are special instances of the overarching Good Gestalt principle, in the sense that being continuous, closed, similar etc. are ways of being maximally good, ordered, simple, etc." (ibid.). Therefore, if the remaining principles which are types of identities are its instances, then it can be concluded that this principle is also based on identity. Todorovic continues: "However, although this idea achieves some explanatory economy and unity, it does so at the cost of clarity and operationalizability: whereas it may be relatively simple to point out the presence of continuity, closure, etc., it is more difficult to establish what exactly makes a pattern visually good, simple, unified, etc." (ibid.). As a reply to this remark of his, it can be said that the thing that makes the 'pattern' visually good, simple, unified, etc. is always some type of identity between the elements which it is created from.

One can conclude that the cognition of visual perceptions, same as the cognition sensations, is governed by the principle of identity and difference, as well as that Gestalt principles for the formation of perceptions are but specific formulations of this basic principle. They are solely different types of identifications. I presume that the same would apply for the auditory and other types of perceptions, i.e. that the elementary sounds and the remaining other sensations the reason unites based on some kind of relation of identity between them.

1.5 Cognition of universals

In this chapter, an attempt will be made to show that universals too are known on the principle of identity and difference. Earlier (in chapter 1.2.2.) it was established that universals are unities of particular or less general things which are united according to a certain common, i.e. identical property. The manner of their creation can be derived directly from this nature of theirs: it is fairly certain that in order to create this types of unities from identical things it is necessary that the reason compares the particular or the less general things, to establish identities and differences between them, and to unite the identical ones in bigger wholes.

Or, more elaborately: the initial processing of material provided by the senses, in the manner described in the previous chapter, results in a large multeity of particular uniformities in themselves, i.e. sensations and perceptions with various specific properties. Identification and differentiation are now being performed on them. As electrical impulses served as data for obtaining sensations and perceptions, so do now sensations and perceptions serve as data for obtaining universals. Each whole, structure, obtained by the unification of the particular things according to identity is a universal, and this is actually the cognitive process of universals. For example, the reason establishes a relation of the identity of solubility and workability between multiple particular things. According to this relation of identity, it unites them under a universal, giving them a single common name – metals. Additionally, between the metals and other universals it establishes a relation of the identity of possessing mass, and according to this, it unites them under a broader universal – matter.[21] What is characteristic here is that identification and differentiation while building the universals does not happen only between things that exist within certain present real time and space which is the case with the sensory and perceptual cognition. On cognition of universals, identification expands to the particular things known in a past time and other places that can exist only in the memory. Hence, memory is important in the creation of universals.

As for the question of their ontological status, which is one aspect of the problem of universals, as it is called in metaphysics, it is clear that the reason carries out the process of identification and differentiation inside our heads between, as it was established earlier, particular mental things, which means that universals, as we know them, are of mental nature and exist in our heads. Philosophers (nominalists) who only recognize the reality of particular things, and contest reality of universals, do not notice that both of these have the same nature and exist in the same way as mental substantivized identities.

There is a potential to create as many universals as there are common properties between things. However, not every relation of identity is substantivized into a universal. Some relations of identity remain only at the level of connections between particular things. For example, a relation of identity can be established between multiple people who wear black shoes and yet we do not create the universal 'blackshoers'. This identity will only remain as a connection between certain people. I presume it depends on the human praxis and pragma whether a relation of identity will be substantivized or not.

It is fairly certain that the particular things are chronologically known before the universals, however, it does not have to mean that the more

---

[21] Interesting is the case with the Aristotelian universal – *categories*. Namely, categories are those universals that do not fall under a broader generic term. Paradoxically, it is precisely that the term 'categories' becomes their generic term that unifies them according to the common property not to have a broader generic term.

broader universals are created chronologically later than the more specific. For example, the universal 'animal' has been created earlier, and the universals 'vertebrates' and 'invertebrates' have been created much later. It is also known that the ancient philosophers recognized the most universal of all terms – being, and the numerous specific beings or creatures were known much later.

As one moves toward bigger and bigger syntheses, their internal unity decreases and their internal diversification increases. And all the way to the broadest universal of all which is characterized with the least internal unity and the largest internal diversification. The oneness is the farthest that the reason can reach: there is no further generalization past the oneness because a generalization requires at least two things and their common property. All things are same because they exist. According to this, the ultimate *identity between* is the universal 'being', which is a unity of all different things according to the common property – existence. Or, one can say that being is a substantivized relation of identity between all different things according to the property of existence. If pure identities in themselves – sensations were denoted the most basic elements of knowledge, then the one, the being, is the most comprehensive *identity between*, the most comprehensive element of knowledge. So, from the numerous identities in themselves of the material provided by the senses, whose essential property is their indivisibility, the reason reaches to their ultimate unification – the being, whose essential property is its inconnectability.

According to this, a universal can be defined as a substantivized content of an identity relation between the concrete things that it encompasses. The essence of the universal is the *identity between* things that belong to it; the identity is the connective tissue that unites concretes under a universal that encompasses them. It is actually its definition. The definition of the universal is the content of the relation of identity. What applies to the creation of sensible things applies to universals too. The creation of the universals is merely a sequel to the process of identity-difference processing, but, now not directly of the material provided by the senses, but on another, a higher level of identity-difference processing of products from the processing of the material provided by the senses. It can be concluded that the reason creates universals on the principle of identity and difference.

****

Many philosophers consider that there is a difference between the cognition of sensible things and cognition of universals. Immanuel Kant falls in this group, and he distinguishes between two kinds of cognition – the faculty of sensibility and the faculty of understanding. However, opposed to these opinions, according to the analysis presented here, it can be noticed that there is no essential difference between these two kinds of cognition. As it was concluded, the cognition of sensations, perceptions, as well as universals, is based on the principle of identity and difference.

The active and creational role of the subject of a cognition that Kant has so brilliantly realized, becomes very clear. Now it is clear that this role consists of comparing by identification and differentiation and appropriate formation of wholes made of identities. In this context, I will cite the initial words of Kant's *Critique of Pure Reason* – the thesis that fits excellently in the system elaborated here:

> There is no doubt whatever that all our cognition begins with experience; for how else should the cognitive faculty be awakened into exercise if not through objects that stimulate our senses and in part themselves produce representations, in part bring the activity of our understanding into motion to compare these, to connect or separate them, and thus to work up the raw material of sensible impressions into a cognition of objects that is called experience? **As far as time is concerned**, then, no cognition in us precedes experience, and with experience every cognition begins. (Kant, 1787, 136)

As it can be seen, Kant explicitly uses the terms 'compare, connect, and separate' when he describes the role of the reason in the cognitive process. The comparing is actually identification and differentiation, and each connection is according to the identification, and each separation is according to differentiation, which is a fantastic overlap with the theory presented here although in the further development of his theory there is a dramatic discrepancy.

Cognition of reality can be understood as weaving a web of identities and differences of the material provided by the senses horizontally in experience and vertically in abstractions. It is an ability to organize the sensory material. The reason possesses such an essential property to understand as oneness everything that it will denote as identical in the material provided by the senses, and to create oneness from multiple identical things. The historical process of development of the knowledge of the world is a process of mapping the identity-difference structure of the totality of the material provided by the senses obtained from all times and all spaces wherein the relations of identity or difference, which remain unchangeable through time, hold a special place. The reason gains knowledge on the principle of identity and difference.

2.
Reason as a thinking subject

Apart from being a cognitive subject, another fundamental appearance of the reason is being a subject that thinks. Thinking is considered a part of the cognitive process, its most meaningful part even, which finalizes knowledge following the cognition of sensations, perceptions, and universals. Thinking refers to the knowledge of propositions. The core of thinking is made of the operations performed by the reason which are generally known as abstract-logical reasoning, and they will be the topic of discussion in this chapter. Those are the methods of cognition, i.e. the shapes of inference, as well as several other operations. They are faces of reason. An attempt will be made to show here that each operation performed by the reason reduces to identification and differentiation, i.e. that the core of each operation of the reason is some kind of identification or differentiation.

2.1 Induction

The induction is a way of thinking, reasoning, i.e. reaching conclusions. When speaking of induction in philosophical literature the problem of the truth value of inductive conclusions is usually the subject of discussion; however, here I am interested in the very essence of this operation of reason. I will try to demonstrate that the induction is essentially a type of identification.

Here is one example of incomplete generalizing induction which will serve as an illustration:

1. Bertrand Russell is mortal
2. Ludwig Wittgenstein is mortal
3. David Hume is mortal
4. John Stuart Mill is mortal
5. .
6. .
7. .
8. N is mortal

All people are mortal

What does actually the reason do at the moment of reaching this conclusion? At first, it identifies between individual people (Russell, Socrates...) according to the property of mortality. Then it identifies, under an assumption, these known cases with the cases of other unknown individuals and as a result, it reaches the conclusion that all people are mortal. According to this, it can be said that induction is a complex process of identification created of two subprocesses – first the identification between individual cases, and then the assumption of the identity of known with unknown cases.

That the induction is identification, it can be seen even from the analysis of its formulations. Maybe the best formulation of induction is given to us by David Hume.[1] Although he himself never uses the term, it is fairly certain that he refers to induction when he claims that it is a principle according to which "...*instances, of which we have had no experience, must resemble those, of which we have had experience, and that the course of nature always continues uniformly the same*" (Hume, 1739 - 40, 62). The keyword in this claim is 'resemble'. It is quite justified to consider resemblance as identity. It is a partial identity, i.e. identity according to one or more of the properties of things whose relation is scrutinized. If one abstracts these properties, the result is pure identity. This abstraction is even more justified since only the property which is the bearer of identity is important to induction or the thinking process in general. Hume's definition can be, accordingly, paraphrased thus: instances of which we have had no experience are identical with those of which we have had experience. Or more elegantly: unknown cases are identical to the known. Now the identification in the background of each induction is obvious. It is an identification between the known and then between the known and unknown cases of the same class according to a certain property.

John Stuart Mill has similar views, he founds induction on the principle of uniformity of nature. According to him, induction can be logically justified only if "...there are such things in nature as parallel cases; that what happens once, will, under a sufficient degree of similarity of circumstances, happen again" (Mill, 1843, 306). On a more in-depth analy-

---

[1] Hume is considered an initiator of the issue with the logical foundation of induction. He concludes that the induction is not an act of reason but of habit, something to which I cannot agree. I believe that this is due to the lack of logical basis of the second subprocess of identification. It seems that Hume tacitly supposes that the reason is perfect. Namely, the mere fact of identification is enough for me to conclude that it is an act of reason, regardless of its truth value and justification. The reason is perfectly capable of errors too.

sis of the stated principle, it will be concluded that actually it claims identity between things that happened once and the things that would happen in the future under a sufficient degree of similarity (identity) of circumstances. Cohen and Nagel offer a slightly different formulation of the same principle, such as: "... same cause will under similar circumstances be accompanied by the same effect" (Cohen and Nagel, 1934, 267). Identity here is much more obvious. Here a relation of identity is claimed between the cause and effect relations in the past and those in the present or the future if the circumstances are similar enough. If Mill founds induction on this principle, he founds induction on identification.

It can be concluded that the induction is a specific identification, i.e. that the essence of the inductive concluding is the operation of identification of the reason.

2.2 Deduction

The deduction is one other way of thinking, i.e. reaching conclusions. The logical shape of a deduction procedure is the syllogism, as it is shown in the following example:

1. *All men are mortal*
2. *Bertrand Russell is a man*
3. *Bertrand Russell is mortal*

We are familiar with the structure of a syllogism; it consists of three basic statements, two premises, and one conclusion. In logic three terms are also distinguished: major, minor, and middle terms. I consider the essential part of the syllogism the fact that the middle term (*terminus medius*) exists in both premises as their common and enables conclusion. The middle term in this example is 'man'. This is actually the term according to which a relation of identity between both premises is established upon, and the conclusion is based on establishing exactly this relation of identity. An attempt will be made at proving this in the pages to follow.

Propositions in logic are defined as sentences to claim or deny something from which their property of being false or true stems. I firmly believe that each statement like this of the kind '*S is (not) P*' actually claims identity or difference between the subject and the predicate, wherein the copula '*is*' means '*is identical as*', while the copula '*is not*' means '*is different than*', but with a very important remark that identity is always partial, i.e. it is based on one or more properties. I presume that logicians known as relationists which reject the traditional formulation 'S (is) not P' and introduce the 'aRb' formula that reads 'a has such and such relation to b', would agree with this view.[2] So, for the first premise in the example given above it can be said that the thing that means 'men' is identical with 'to be mortal' in the sense that mortality as property is one of the properties of men. Additionally, the second premise can be said to be 'Bertrand Russell is identical with man' in the sense that the properties covered by the universal 'man' are identical with part of the properties of the individual Bertrand Russell. Same goes for the conclusion of the syllogism. When we utter a predicate for a certain subject, when we describe it, we do so according to identification. The predicate belongs to the subject because it is partially identical to it. The predicate is a known universal to us, and with the known, we identify the unknown, that is, the subject that we want to describe.

There are similar opinions in the Megarian-Stoic logician Stilpo who claimed that "only the identical judgments can be stated and that according to that the statements have one form only "A is (not) A"' (Josifovski, 1984, 99). Aside from Stilpo and according to the most famous medieval scholastic logician, Abelard, "the connection "is" represents a symbol for the identity of the subject and the predicate" (Josifovski, 1984, 124).

At first glance this opinion seems 'forced', and it would be accepted best if the subject and the predicate are represented as sets of properties[3] or modes of comparison they possess. Then, for every true statement 'S is P' there will be an element in 'S' completely identical to 'P'. It will be possible for each statement of the 'S is P' kind to be represented as an intersection of the two sets. Forcedness stems from the fact that we are dealing here with a partial identity, which is harder to be established as opposed to the usual abstract understanding of identity as absolute.[4] Of course one cannot speak of absolute identity, only partial. If one insists on absolute identity, then even statements such as 'the pencil is red' become disputable, as in the following reasoning: A pencil is a material object, red is an abstract idea. How can we then claim that the pencil is red? Are we claiming that a pencil is an abstract idea?

---

[2] In relationist logic there is a problem with classification of relations. As a possible contribution toward the solution of this problem, I would say that both fundamental kinds of relations are identity and difference, and all other relations represent specific identities or differences between different things and according to different properties.

[3] Support for these views is found in Bertrand Russell who claims that "a "thing,, is nothing but a bundle of coexisting qualities" (Russell, 1940, p. 97)

[4] More about this distinction follows later in this chapter.

So, now the syllogism would acquire the following, almost acceptable linguistic form:
1. Being a man is identical to being mortal
2. Bertrand Russell is identical to man
3. Bertrand Russell is identical to being mortal

Let us replace with symbols: all men = A; mortal = B; Bertrand Russell = C

$A=B$
$\underline{C=A}$
$C=B$

In this way, a simple equation is obtained from which it can be easily seen that the process of deductive thinking includes a series of identifications, first between the subject and the predicate from the first and second premises. Then the main identification, the essence of the deduction, between the two premises according to the middle term, wherein, with the application of Euclid's rule: 'Things equal to the same thing are also equal to one another', as a conclusion we get identity between the major and the minor term. The deduction is the usage of the transitivity of identity.

Another argument for additional support of the thesis presented here can be found through the analysis of the 'dictum de omni et nullo' maxim which according to John Stuart Mill is the fundament of deductive reasoning: "The maxim is, That whatever can be affirmed (or denied) of a class, may be affirmed (or denied) of everything included in the class. This axiom, supposed to be the basis of the syllogistic theory, is termed by logicians the *dictum de omni et nullo*" (Mill, 1843, 174). Identity is the essence of this maxim because what is affirmed or denied of the class and each of its members, as it is the case with propositions, is what the class and its member are identical upon. Having considered this, one can say that each affirmation is the identification and each negation is differentiation as a confirmation of the thesis presented above that each logical statement claims identity or difference.

From all of the above one can conclude that identity is the fundamental principle of deductive reasoning. The essence of the deductive conclusion is the operation of identification by the reason, that is, the deduction is a specific identification.

****

In the logical theory, "a distinction is customarily drawn between qualitative and numerical identity or sameness. Things with qualitative identity share properties so that things can be more or less qualitatively identical" (Noonan, Harold and Curtis, intro). Bertrand Russell and Ludwig Wittgenstein are qualitatively identical because they share the property of being a man, and such properties as go along with that. On the other hand "Numerical identity requires absolute, or total, qualitative identity, and can only hold between a thing and itself." (Noonan, Harold and Curtis, intro). Actually, qualitative identity is the one that I called it - partial while numerical identity is another name for the absolute identity. The identity is a type of relation. The very concept of relation implies the existence of at least two things. Therefore, I reckon it is meaningless talking about a relation of only one thing, i.e. for the relation of the thing to itself. Such a relation can only be created by artificial duplication of the thing in our thoughts. Further, if we talk about two things, then they must be at least in something different; the very fact that there are two, and not one, indicates that they are different; there are no two things that are absolutely identical. This conclusion is actually Leibniz's Law - The Identity of Indiscernibles: „It states that no two distinct things exactly resemble each other. ...and is typically understood to mean that no two objects have exactly the same properties" (Forrest, intro). And not only that there are no two things that are absolutely identical, but also there are no two things that are absolutely different. Two things are identical at least because they both exist and, if not in reality, then they are identical because they exist in our thoughts. According to that, every identity is partial identity, according to a certain property of things that compare, and whenever we claim identity or difference, we have some comparison mode in mind. I am convinced that these ideas will correspond with the radical ideas of the English philosopher Peter Geach: "I am arguing for the thesis that identity is relative. When one says "x is identical with y", this I hold, is incomplete expression; it is short for "x is the same A as y", where "A" represents some count noun understood from the context of utterance- or else, it is just a vague expression of a half-formed thought" (Geach, 1972, 238).

2.3 Analogy

Analogy as a method of reasoning is considered the fundamental ability of the human reason. Hofstadter defines it as the "core of the cognition" (Gentner, Holyoak and Kokinov, 2001, 499-538). Except as a method of reasoning, which would be a type of operation of reason, an analogy can be understood as a result of reasoning, which would be a type of relation established by reason. First and foremost analogy will be discussed as an operation of reason, and an attempt will be made to demonstrate that in its essence it is merely an identification process. Further analogy will be analyzed as a result, and an attempt will be made to prove that in its essence it is an identity. The arguments supporting the thesis presented here will be mostly derived from the analysis of analogy definitions in philosophy made by authorities.

According to the definition in Stanford Encyclopedia of Philosophy, "An *analogy* is a comparison between two objects or systems of objects that highlight respects in which they are thought to be **similar**. ...An *analogical argument* is an explicit representation of a form of analogical reasoning that cites accepted **similarities** between two systems to support the conclusion that some further **similarity** exists (Emphasis Mine)" (Bartha, entry).

The key term in these two claims is 'similar', and if it is replaced by the term 'identity' without changing their meaning, they will become a direct confirmation of the thesis presented here. This replacement is completely justified because the similarity is a partial identity or a synonym of identity. For example, we say that fish and whales are similar. If we abstract the essence of similarity, which in this case, among the others, is living underwater, we will obtain pure identity: fish and whales are identical according to the property of living underwater. The confirmation for the justification of the replacement of similarity with identity can be found in Paul Bartha's analysis of Aristotle's theory of analogy. Namely, he sums up four important criteria for evaluation of analogous arguments, and one of them is the following: "*Similarity reduces to identical properties and relations*" (Bartha, para. 3.2). This is exactly what I am looking for.[5]

According to this, the first definition could read as follows: An *analogy* is a comparison between two objects, or systems of objects, that highlights respects in which they are thought to be identical. The comparison mentioned here implies identification and differentiation, and the part of the statement 'highlights respects in which they are thought to be identical' points to us that exactly the noted identity between the two objects allows us to make the analogy. Therefore, it can be said that analogy is in its essence identification between two objects, or systems of objects.

As for the second definition, it can be interpreted like this: Analogical reasoning is reasoning which based on the accepted identities between two systems to support the conclusion that some further identities exist. For example:

---

[5] Previously, on elaborating the Gestalt principle for the formulation of perceptions based on similarities and during the analysis of Hume's definition of induction, I claimed that similarity is reduced to an identity. Let this explanation serve as a support of those theses.

In 1934, the pharmacologist Schaumann was testing synthetic compounds for their anti-spasmodic effect. These drugs had a chemical structure similar to morphine. He observed that one of the compounds—*meperidine*, also known as *Demerol*—had a physical effect on mice that was previously observed only with morphine: it induced an S-shaped tail curvature. By analogy, he conjectured that the drug might also share morphine's narcotic effects. Testing on rats, rabbits, dogs, and eventually humans, showed that meperidine, like morphine, was an effective painkiller (qtd. in Bartha, para. 2.1).

The accepted identities in this example are according to the chemical structure, that is, segments of the chemical structure, as well as on the physical effect on the mice. Based on these identities it is concluded that there is another relation of identity between morphine and meperidine according to the narcotic effect. From here it is clear that the analogical reasoning is founded on identification. Considering the probable truthfulness of this type of conclusion, it would be more accurate to say that analogy is probable identification between two objects or systems of objects. However, the issue with the justification of this type of conclusion is secondary to our discussion.

Except as an operation of reason, an analogy can also be understood as a relation stemming from analogical reasoning. An attempt will be made to demonstrate that understood like this analogy is a specific type of identity relation. First of all, its etymological definition points to this understanding. Namely "In logic, authors were aware that the Greek word 'αναλογια', sometimes called *'analogia'* in Latin, but often translated as *'proportio'* or *'proportionalitas'*, referred to the comparison between two proportions" (Ashworth, para. 3). Proportions are relations, therefore in this sense analogy is a relation of relations. Kant accepted this understanding, if one judges by this quote of his from *Prolegomena*: "This type of cognition is cognition according to analogy, which surely does not signify, as the word is usually taken, an imperfect similarity between two things, but rather a perfect similarity between two relations in wholly dissimilar things" (Kant, 1783, §58, 108). The analogy in this case is not a 'simple' relation between two things, but a relation between relations or a metarelation. It is fairly easy to reduce thusly understood analogy to identity. Here is one example in the spirit of this understanding: darkness to light is analogous to silence to sound. Darkness and light are opposite things or, the relation between light and darkness is an opposition. Silence and sound are also opposite things and the relation between the two is opposition. So, when claiming that darkness to light is analogous to silence to sound, an identity between relations is claimed – opposition is identical to the opposition. Or, a different example: the mouse to the cat is just like the fly to the spider. The relation, in this case, is prey, and the identification is performed according to it: prey is like prey, that is, prey is identical to prey.

Another argument in support of the thesis presented here is found in the Canadian researcher Cameron Shelley. He informs us that "most current theories of analogy make essentially the same claims about what an analogy is. These theories can collectively be called *shared-structure* theories because they emphasize the presence of *mappings* or alignments of hierarchically structured, *causal* relationships shared between source and target analogs" (Shelley, 2003, 6 - 7). If the source and target analogues share the structure, this means that they are identical according to the structure which once again confirms the thesis of identity as the essence of analogy presented here. The achievement of this identity, which also means the creation of analogy, can be made only through the identification and according to that identification represents a fundament in the analogical reasoning.

The term 'shared' is not essential only to the most current theories of analogy as it can be seen from the sketch of the history of theories of analogy made by Shelley. He divides theories of analogy in three types "the *shared-abstraction* theories of Plato and Aristotle, the *shared-attribute* theories of Bacon and Mill, and the shared-structure theories developed in the 20th century" (Shelley, 2003, 137). According to this, the reasoning above applies to the theories of Plato and Aristotle, as well as to the theories of Bacon and Mill. Regardless if the identity is between abstractions, attributes, or structures it still is an identity which is the only important thing for the thesis presented here.

In a different meaning, Douglas Hofstadter and his team identify analogy with a higher level of perception. Without the intention to delve deeper into the specifics of their theory I will only present one of their citations that is a striking confirmation of my thesis: "When people make analogies, they are perceiving some aspects of the structures of two situations—the *essences* of those situations, in some sense—as identical" (Chalmers, French & Hofstadter, 1991, 10-11). Identity as the essence of the analogy is stated here directly. Namely, in this case, analogy is explained as an identity between certain aspects of the structures of two situations.

There is a wonderful video example (Cabrera Research Lab, 2008)[6] which shows the relation between metaphor, simile, and analogy. The author claims that each metaphor and each simile have an analogy in their structure which he considers the core of cognition. I will paraphrase the video here: if we say that the car is a bullet, we are making a metaphor; if we say that the car is like a bullet, we are making a simile, a statement that points out how two things are similar in some way; if we say that the car is like the bullet, that is, that the car is as fast as the bullet, this is an analogy. However, I would not agree with the claim that analogy is the core of cognition because we can go even deeper and in the same manner claim that each metaphor, simile, and analogy has an identity in its structure. The identity in this specific example is according to the property of speed. The car is fast, the bullet is fast – fast is identical to fast. And exactly this identification is the essence of analogy, simile, and metaphor in this case. The core of cognition is the identification and differentiation, and simile, metaphor, and analogy are merely their variations. It can be concluded that analogy as an operation of reason is in its essence identification, and analogy understood as a relation is a type of identity relation.

2.4 Analysis

The analysis is one of the manners of thinking. In this chapter, through a kind of analysis of the analysis, an attempt will be made to demonstrate that it is in fact based on identification and differentiation.

A multiety of conceptions of analysis are known in the history of philosophy, and it is hard to tell if there is any general consensus on its definition. According to one definition analysis is a process of decomposition of something to its constituents which hints at the mechanical separation of a complex object to its constituents. However, when we are discussing the analysis of terms (concepts), decomposition can be understood only at a metaphorical level, as was precisely noted by Quine (1963, 20 - 21). When we are discussing the analysis of terms, then it is hard to differentiate between its constituents with the same precision. Analysis is in fact decomposition as much as the properties of a certain object, which are in fact universal, can be understood as its constituents.

This definition of analysis, also known as decompositional conception, became widespread with the scientific revolution in the seventeenth century, and its roots can be traced back as early as Plato and his searches for definitions. Term analysis is a type of decompositional analysis. For

---

[6] See the link in bibliography

example, the term 'gold' is analyzed (decomposed) to the terms chemical element and workability. What is the background of this process of the reason? In this case first, we have identification between the term 'gold' and the term 'chemical element' because the gold molecules are made of identical atoms just like the molecules of chemical elements. This is the property that defines the term 'chemical element'. Or, more elegantly, according to this property, the gold is identical to a chemical element. Then we have identification of gold with the term 'workability'. Workability represents changing the shape and dimensions of materials without splitting of particles. The shape and dimensions of gold can be changed without splitting of particles. All in all, decompositional analysis consists of identification of the object of analysis with one or more other terms.[7] This example is more appropriate to the intentional definition of the generic term and specific difference. On the other hand, the pure analysis of a term is a simple identification of the subject of the analysis to other terms. For example, the pure formally logical analysis of the term 'man' consists of revealing and simple listing of its elementary properties: living being, two-legged, reasonable being, etc.

Another conception of analysis known as regressive conception according to which "'analysis' referred primarily to the process of working back to first principles by means of which something could then be demonstrated" (Beaney, para. 1.1) was predominant in antiquity. In another sense, it can be understood as a process of working back from theorems to axioms or from effects to causes. This definition, however, is pretty general and vague and identification as its essence can be hardly recognized in it. Therefore I think that the best way to show the reduction in this type of analysis to identification/differentiation is through a concrete example. Here is an excerpt from Euclid's geometry, an ingenious proof which is considered a classic example of regressive analysis understood as a process of working back from theorems to axioms:

> Proposition 47.
> In right-angled triangles, the square on the side subtending the right angle is equal to the squares on the sides containing the right angle.
> Let ABC be a right-angled triangle having the angle BAC right; I say that the square on BC is equal to the squares on BA, AC. For let, there be described on BC the square BDEC, and on BA, AC the squares GB, HC; through A let AL be drawn parallel to either BD or

---

[7] These examples can also be used as illustration of the identity between the subject and the predicate of which was discussed in the chapter of deduction.

CE and let AD, FC be joined. Then, since each of the angles BAC, BAG is right, it follows that with a straight line BA, and at the point A on it, the two straight lines AC, AG not lying on the same side make the adjacent angles equal to two right angles; therefore CA is in a straight line with AG. For the same reason, BA is also in a straight line with AH. And, since the angle DBC is equal to the angle FBA: for each is right: let the angle ABC be added to each; therefore the whole angle DBA is equal to the whole angle FBC. And, since DB is equal to BC, and FB to BA, the two sides AB, BD are equal to the two sides FB, BC respectively ; and the angle ABD is equal to the angle FBC ; therefore the base AD is equal to the base FC, and the triangle ABD is equal to the triangle FBC. Now the parallelogram BL is double of the triangle ABD, for they have the same base BD and are in the same parallels BD, AL. And the square GB is double of the triangle FBC, for they again have the same base FB and are on the same parallels FB, GC. [But the doubles of equals are equal to one another.] Therefore the parallelogram BL is also equal to the square GB. Similarly, if AE, BK be joined, the parallelogram CL can also be proved equal to the square HC; therefore the whole square BDEC is equal to the two squares GB, HC. And the square BDEC is described on BC, and the squares GB, HC on BA, AC. Therefore the square on the side BC is equal to the squares on the sides BA, AC. (Euclid, book 1, 349-350)

What exactly does the reason do in the course of this proving process? Pay attention to the word 'equal' which is mentioned a total of fifteen times and the word 'same' which is mentioned a total of six times. Both, the phrase 'is equal' and the word 'same' used here denote a relation of identity, and everywhere the words 'equal' or 'same' are used there is an identification between elements. According to this, it can be concluded that the so-called process of working back consists of series of identifications and that if this excerpt represents regressive analysis, then the regressive analysis is essentially identification and differentiation.[8]

Identification as a fundamental principle has not gone unnoticed in Euclid, although this is not explicitly stated. His 'common notions' at the

---

[8] I hold onto identification and differentiation since these two operations of reason always go hand in hand in a dialectical cohesion. If a deep enough analysis is performed on the activity of the reason it will be concluded that each identification of things is at the same time differentiation from other things, and vice versa, although usually only identification is stated.

beginning of the *Elements*, along with the axioms, attest to this. These are the first four of a total of five 'common notions'[9] of Euclid's *Elements*:

1. Things which are equal to the same thing are also equal to one another.
2. If equals are added to equals, the wholes are equal.
3. If equals are subtracted from equals, the remainders are equal.
4. Things which coincide with one another are equal to one another. (op. cit. 155)

Algebra also called the 'art of analysis', is also considered an example of regressive analysis. It is enough that we understand the symbol '=' as a relation of identity to conclude that the 'art of analysis' is essentially a skill to identify and differentiate among quantities. And not only in algebra but also in mathematics generally, i.e. everywhere where the symbol '=' exists it is actually a matter of identification.

G. E. Moore set the so-called paradox of analysis which can be traced back to antiquity, from Plato's *Meno*. According to him, analysis cannot be accurate and informative at the same time. Here is how Michael Beaney formulated the paradox:

> "Consider an analysis of the form "A is C", where A is the *analysandum* (what is analysed) and C the *analysans* (what is offered as the analysis). Then either "A" and "C" have the same meaning, in which case the analysis expresses a trivial identity; or else they do not, in which case the analysis is incorrect. So it would seem that no analysis can be both correct and informative." (Beaney, para. 6, Supplement para. 4)[10]

Let us first note that this citation confirms that the analysis is based on identification because it clearly claims identity according to the meaning of *analysandum* and *analysans*. As to the paradox, I consider that the informativeness or usefulness of the analysis, at least one of its aspects, consists of reduction of the complex unobvious identity to simple and obvious identity. For example, we know that this algebraic expression '4x+3x2−x+2=38' contains the value of an unknown, that is, the number with which the unknown is identical with, however, this identity is unob-

---

[9] These 'common notions' of Euclid can seriously rival the classical logical laws on the epithet laws of thinking.

[10] See the following link: <http://plato.stanford.edu/archives/win2015/entries/analysis/s6.html>.

vious. If the problem is solved,[11] that is, if its analysis is performed, one does not acquire new knowledge, but the only transformation of the unobvious identity into obvious: $x = -4.3$. The difference between the algebraic expression that we know as a problem and the one that is a solution consists only of their complexness, that is, obviousness, wherein the solution is considered the simplest and the most obvious expression of identity. In general, it can be said that the usefulness of the analysis consists of the transformation of the complex into simple, unknown into known, unobvious into obvious. This transformation could be considered a possible contribution to the solution of the paradox. Another aspect of the usefulness of the analysis stems from the partial character of identity between *analysandum* and *analysans*. Trivial and absolute identity is the identity of a thing with itself. Each other identity is partial and with that informative and nontrivial.

Of all these arguments offered, it can be concluded that analysis is based on the identification.

2.5 Association

"It is evident, that there is a principle of connexion between the different thoughts or ideas of the mind, and that, in their appearance to the memory or imagination, they introduce each other with a certain degree of method and regularity" (Hume, 1748, 16). With this sentence, Hume opens his elaboration on the association of ideas. In this chapter, an attempt will be made to demonstrate that the principle of 'connexion', which he speaks of, is in fact identity.

Association is an operation of reason, another manner of existence of the reason, so to speak. It is the basic mechanism with which the functioning of memory, as well as the process of learning, are explained as appearances of reason. Aside from that, there are attempts in philosophy and psychology, more precisely in English empiricists, to explain the complete mental activity through associations, which speaks of their depth and fundamentality. The roots of this theory, also known as associationism, can be traced all the way back to Antiquity in Plato and Aristotle. In the recent history of philosophy, among others, associationists are considered Hobbes, Berkeley, Hume, and Hamilton; while this theory was deepened through the work of David Hartley, Priestley, James Mill,

---

[11] Let us note that the transformation, that is, the solving of the problem is performed according to the laws on which algebra is based (commutative, associative, and distributive) which are also in their essence identities which always apply, regardless of the value of variables.

John Stuart Mill, Bain, Spencer, and others. These ideas are shared by behavioristic as well as other modern connectivistic theoreticians of thought.

Associationism is a broad constellation of theories, and I consider the best and the shortest way to prove my thesis is through analysis of principles of the association since they constitute the very essence of the theory. Different thinkers define different principles, therefore there is no general accord regarding this issue. I shall begin with Aristotle.

Researchers derive Aristotelian principles of association from a not so clear paragraph of his *On Memory*:

> Whenever, therefore, we are recollecting, we are experiencing one of the antecedent movements until finally, we experience the one after which customarily comes that which we seek. This explains why we hunt up the series, having started in thought from the present or some other, and from something either similar, or contrary, to what we seek, or else from that which is contiguous with it. That is how recollection takes place; for the movements involved in these starting-points are in some cases identical, in others, again, simultaneous, while in others they comprise a portion of them, so that the remnant which one experienced after that portion is comparatively small. (*On Memory*, 451b17 – 25)

Isolated principles are usually known as contiguity, similarity, and contrast, and it can be said that all future research of the associations is based on them.

Following Aristotle, the first philosopher that tries to categorize associations is David Hume. He writes: "To me, there appear to be only three principles of connexion among ideas, namely, *Resemblance, Contiguity* in time or place, and *Cause* or *Effect*" (Hume, 1748, 16). To the great significance that he attributed to these principles testifies one of his citations with which he concludes the *abstract* toward his *Treatise of Human Nature*:

> 'Twill be easy to conceive of what vast consequence these principles must be in the science of human nature, if we consider, that so far as regards the mind, these are the only links that bind the parts of the universe together, or connect us with any person or object exterior to ourselves. For as it is by means of thought only that any thing operates upon our passions, and as these are the only ties of our thoughts, they are really to us the cement of the

universe, and all the operations of the mind must, in a great measure, depend on them. (Hume, 1739 – 40, 416 - 417)

Aside from these, there are many other attempts to determine and categorize the principles of association or connection of ideas, and as it was already said, there is no general consensus between associationists regarding the principles of association. Other principles are also suggested, and also there are known attempts for these principles to be reduced to even more fundamental ones. Most frequent are the attempts to reduce all the principles to similarity or contiguity which are also considered the most generally accepted. Here, in a similar manner, I will try to reduce these most generally accepted principles of association to one and only principle of identity.

It can be said that this principle already exists in theory, only under a different name, that is, as a principle of similarity, because the similarity in its essence is, in fact, an identity. It is recognized by almost all theoreticians in this domain as one of the most important principles. This fact greatly simplifies the task at hand. The usual formulation of the principle of similarity is the following: "An experience tends to recall experiences which resemble it" (Warren, 1921, 283). Or, in a different formulation: one idea associates to another idea which is similar to it. On several occasions previously it was demonstrated that each similarity could be abstracted to pure identity. One idea is similar to another if there are one or more identical properties and the more identical properties they share, the greater their similarity. Association is due exactly to the identical properties.

The second generally accepted principle of association is contiguity. According to the definition of the American psychologist Howard Warren, the principle of contiguity implies that "A sensation or idea tends to recall other experiences which formerly occurred in close proximity to it" (ibid.). Next, an attempt will be made to demonstrate that the 'proximity' actually means belonging to an identical sequence of experiences and according to this the principle can be reduced to identity.

The very term 'contiguity' is not specific enough. It can mean identity according to time and/or space of existence, and in other definitions, it can mean proximity in space and/or time. If the meaning of 'contiguity' is understood as existence at the same time and/or space of both things that are associated, then the reduction to identity is obvious. However, this reduction obviously does not apply to the things which are proximal only in space and/or time. Additional, and maybe the most problematic, unclarity stems from the relativity of the term 'proximity'. If, for example,

I recollect an event which happened during summer many years ago, then this event can associate itself with another meaningful event from the same summer which would be in temporal proximity of one or two months. On the other hand, if I recollect an event from yesterday, it can associate itself with another event from yesterday with temporal proximity of one or two hours. In theory, this problem, relating to the determination of parameters needed for proximity, is sometimes known as the problem of the 'Window of Association'. In the end, it is not quite clear why exactly contiguity is so important as a relation to the course of our thoughts, that is, to the association, between all the other properties and relations they have?

One way of surpassing these unclarities and at the same time reducing this principle to identity is to understand contiguous things as things that exist in the same time and/or space and according to that, as things which are identical according to space and/or the time in which they belong. One can argue that in this case we are simply not talking about the same space and/or time but of proximity in space and/or time, of neighboring or of bordering. And indeed, speaking in strictest terms, two things can be at the same time, but two things cannot be in the same place at the same time. On the other hand, we are witnessing the everyday use of the phrases 'same space (place)' and 'same time', that is, the ascribing of these properties to things. For example, we can claim that the two of us occupy the same place, meaning the room or in another context, the city in which we are located at the moment.

Philosophers and psychologists working on this problem are aware that certain close things are experiences as part of a single sequence of experience. The room and the city from the example above are such single sequences of experience. Howard Warren backs this thesis when he says that: "Sensations which occur contiguously - that is, either simultaneously or in immediate sequence - tend to unite into single experiences or unbroken chains of experience" (op. cit., 285). Hence, things perceived in this way will be identical according to the belonging to the same sequence of experience on which their mutual association would be founded on. This is the wanted reduction of contiguity to identity. However, it is unclear how and why we experience it as such. According to Warren, this is the fundamental problem of the associationism. He writes: "How comes it, then, those coexistent or successive elements are *experienced together* in one complex, unitary experience? This is the fundamental problem of the associationists" (op. cit., 128). In an attempt to make things more clear, let us remind ourselves of the first chapter of this book where it was established that the reason processes the material provided by the senses on the principle of identity and difference, that is, divides space and time into sequences which are uniform in themselves according to one or more properties. Hence, in these specific examples, the room is a spatial sequence uniform in itself according to the emptiness it encompasses as opposed to the material walls around it, the city is uniform in itself according to the buildings as opposed to the nature that surrounds it and so on. For all the things which are within the boundaries of a uniform spatial sequence, one can argue that they are located in the same space and associate with one another/each other on the basis of this identity. They are associated as a part from the same whole, and can also be associated as part of a whole, and vice versa for the part is identical to a part of the whole. In fact, the principle of part-whole has already been proposed by some associationists as a principle of association.

If, for example, we notice a hat like the one our friend has in a window it is highly probable that the perception of the hat in that window will associate to our friend. It is clear that the hat and the friend are not identical things neither in shape, nor color, or according to many other internal properties of theirs. However, this association will take place, since in our past experience the friend and his hat touch in the space creating a unique spatial whole, and they also touch in time because they exist and we perceive them in the same time and in this way they create a unique sequence of experience which is singled out in our reason as a separate whole. The association between the hat and our friend will occur based on their identity according to the belonging to this unique whole in memory. Experiencing each of the other things that belong to that whole is a possible association to our friend and vice versa.

As an illustration to the principle of proximity Hume offers the following example: "The mention of one apartment in a building naturally introduces an enquiry or discourse concerning the others" (Hume, 1748, 16-17). Here it is unclear why one apartment would not associate to another apartment because simply they are both identical according to a certain property that the apartment as a universal possesses or according to the fact that they are both identical according to the belonging to the single sequence of experience, that is, the same building.

Same arguments stand for touching in time. We divide time in uniform sequences according to a certain property. The division into sequences can be of purely 'subjective' nature, as for example: while I was in that room, while I was speaking to that person, while I was surprised, scared, etc. or, of 'objective' nature: that day, that summer, while it rained, etc. All things that happened, that is, that belong to temporal sequences such as these can associate to one another. For example, song verse will associate us with the remaining verse not because they are proximal in time, but because they belong to the identical sequence of experience, in this case, a song. This would be the reduction of time contiguity to identity. Aside from this, two things can simply be at the same time and associate according to this identity.

This is a good explanation to the unclarities mentioned above, that stem from the relativity of the term 'proximity'. It is simply a matter of greater or smaller temporal or spatial sequences, that is, single sequences of experience. The summer is a greater single sequence of experience which is uniform in itself according to the high temperatures and other properties, and the day is a smaller single sequence of experience which is uniform in itself above all, according to the presence of sunlight, continuous awakeness of the subject, etc. All things belonging to these sequences of experience are possible associations because they are identical according to the time and/or place of existence.

As to the causality as a principle of association, it can be categorized into two types: causality where the causes and effects are simultaneous and causality where there is a certain time interval between the cause and the effect. The first type of causality is easily reduced to identity according to the time of occurrence. Characteristic of the second type of causality is that it can form associative relation only through multiple repetitions of the experience. Hume based causality on habit and habit is based on repetition of experience. Repetition is reduced to identity between various temporal sequences in the experience which enables them to be united in a unique whole in our memory. Identity between the cause and the effect according to the belonging to a unique memory whole is the basis for this type of association.

It can be concluded that the only principle of association to which all other reduce is identity. The relation between the wagons of Hume's train of thinking is identity and according to this, association, as one of the reason's operations, is identification in its essence.

2.6 Abstraction

Abstraction is another operation and a manner of appearance of reason. It is by definition "supposed process of forming an idea by abstracting out what is common to a variety of instances" (Blackburn, 1996). Common properties are in fact the content of the identity relation between the variety of instances. In order for the reason to extract these common properties it needs to perform identification, therefore, defined thus, abstraction is, in fact, a procedure for identification between specific examples and their unification, according to the principle of identity and difference, in a whole – a generalized idea or a concept. These generalized ideas and concepts are actually the product of abstraction, and their definition is the content of the identity relation. Hence, properties differentiating between objects of comparison are rejected. This is the other side of the process, and this is why abstraction is often defined as neglect of 'unimportant' properties.

The specification is an operation opposite to abstraction. If abstraction is defined as an act of identification through which we are able to reach the unknown general from the known given specific, specification is then an act of identification through which we are able to reach the unknown specific from the known given general. Of course, the identity between the general and the specific is only partial and can be best portrayed as the identity between a subset and a set, wherein the specification is understood as a set of properties while the general is its subset which consists of at least one property.

It can be concluded that abstraction and specification as operations of reason are actually identifications between generalities and specificities in two directions, that is, that the ability for abstract thinking is reduced to the ability of identification and differentiation.

2.7 Generalization

Generalization is another fundamental manner of appearance of reason. In logic, "Universal generalization (or universal introduction) is the rule of inference that allows one to move from a particular statement to the universal generalization of that statement" (Cook, 2009, 300). In order to move from a particular statement to the universal generalization of that statement, one must identify particularly with universal. Also, "Existential generalization (or existential introduction) is the rule of inference that allows one to move from a particular statement to an existential generalization of that statement" (Cook, 2009, 111). In order to move from a particular statement to an existential generalization of that statement, one must identify particular with the most abstract universal – existence. For example, if we generalize from 'Bertrand Russell is mortal' to 'Someone is mortal' then we are actually identifying particular Bertrand Russell with the universal someone.

According to another definition, generalization is "the process of formulating general concepts by abstracting common properties of instances."[12] The process of abstraction, in this case, is also considered a neces-

---

[12] Retrieved December 19, 2015 from <http://www.vocabulary.com/dictionary/generalization>.

sary predecessor to generalization. Abstraction of the common properties of specificities is a prerequisite for us to be able, to sum up those properties in a general concept, although there is an impression that the difference between these two operations is not entirely clear. Its definition, however, like with abstraction above, clearly points to identification as its essence.

2.8 Categorization

Categorization is by definition "The action or process of placing into classes or groups."[13] Also, the term 'classification' is its synonym, which by definition is "The action or process of classifying something."[14] Or, in biology, "The arrangement of animals and plants in taxonomic groups according to their observed similarities."[15] This process of separating items is actually based on similarities and differences. The key term in these claims is 'similar' which, as it was seen earlier, can be easily abstracted to identity. One can conclude, accordingly, that each categorization and each classification occur according to a certain identity and as such, these are essentially operations of identification and differentiation.

2.9 Definition

Each definition is a relation of identity according to the meanings of the *definiens* and *definiendum*. The process of definition, accordingly, is essentially a process of identification.

****

It can be concluded that the operations of reason discussed so far are often intertwined with one another, making it difficult to identify them in certain cases properly. Establishing the differences and the relations between these operations will not be the topic of discussion here since solely important is the identity between them which is, in fact, an explanation for their intertwining. A sufficient number of operations of reason were considered so far which were also sufficiently fundamental and general for the adoption of the following inductive conclusion: each

---

[13] "categorization, n." *OED Online*, Oxford University Press, June 2017, https://en.oxforddictionaries.com/definition/categorization. Accessed 30 December 2017.

[14] "classification, n." *OED Online*, Oxford University Press, June 2017, https://en.oxforddictionaries.com/definition/classification . Accessed 30 December 2017.

[15] ibid

operation of reason is essentially identification, but it should be noted that identification implies differentiation at the same time.

Identification and differentiation as operations are opposites in dialectical relation: Each identification is at the same time differentiation, and each differentiation is at the same time identification, just like, for example, each labeling is at the same time denying. Any identification, according to one or more properties, is at the same time differentiation according to the other properties of the things that compare. Exactly this distinction is making the comparison possible and thus enables the very identification. The emphasis is on identification because of only its result – identity, means positive knowledge and truth.

This postulate results from the fact that for each identification it is needed for us to know a minimum of two things, and with the very fact that we know two things implies that these two things have to be different by something. In reality, there are no two absolutely identical things, and there are no two absolutely different things. Between any two real things there has to be a difference, and between any two real things, there has to be identity. If nothing else they will be identical according to the fact that they exist and they will be different according to the time and/or space in which they exist. This is why when I talk about identity I always mean a partial identity, and when I talk about differences, I talk about the partial difference.

Parts of these operations are known for they serve as methods for the creation and explanation of the universals which asserts the conclusion that universals are created on the principle of identity and difference. Another part constitutes our ability to come to and elaborate on our judgments and conclusions.

Finally, the thought process consisting of these operations would not be thinking at all if it does not abide by the laws of logic, and as we know, the first of the traditional laws of logic is no other than the law of identity (*Ens est ens*). Although, I disagree with the traditional view of identity as an absolute and, as I said above, I consider that every identity is partial (or relative). I consider that the very fact that the absolute identity can only hold between a thing and itself shows us that it is an absurd relation, fruitless and uninformative tautology which has no application in practical logic. Peter Geach comes to such conclusion and says: „the notion of absolute identity has no application and that there is only relative identity" (Noonan, Harold and Curtis, chapter 3). He claims that „...we should jettison the classical notion of identity"(Noonan, Harold and Curtis, intro). I consider it scandalous to be claimed that the logic rests on a law that actually does not have any practical application. The law of contradiction (*A is not not-A*) can be by all means called law of difference since it claims that 'A' and 'not-A' have to be different, while the law of excluded middle can be reformulated in the following manner: two things are either same or different (in a certain sense). From all of the above, it can be concluded that the fundamental principle of thinking is the principle of identity and difference, that is, that thinking is the ability to identify and differentiate.

3.
Reason as a logical subject – truth

The truth was one of the major topics in philosophy since its very beginnings thousands of years ago, and it still is today. The problem of truth can be easily established: What is the truth? As opposed to its establishing, the attempts at its solving are all but simple. Truth is the central term of one of the most striking forms of the existence of reason – logic, and therefore its investigation in a work that strives to explain the principle of reason functioning is inevitable.

As postulated in logic, the goal of the abstract logical thinking is reaching the truth. In the previous chapter, it was concluded that each form of the abstract logical thinking is essentially identification. The goal and the result of the operation of identification can only be identity, and according to this, the truth is nothing else but a relation of identity and when the reason recognizes truth it actually recognizes a relation of identity. This is the primary thesis and an attempt at proving it will be presented in the first part of this chapter. Existing theories from philosophical authorities will be used to defend this thesis; first and foremost these will be the theory of identity and the theory of correspondence.

The complexity of the problem of truth mainly consists of ontological questions and relates to the ontological status of elements from whose relation the truth results; in modern theory, these are known as truth-bearers and truth-makers. The thesis about to be proven here with its high level of abstractness enables us to set aside this ontological aspect of the problem since regardless of the ontological solution, the truth will remain pure relation of identity in its essence, irrespective of the entities between which the said relation will be established. However, this proposed answer to the 'What is truth' question, as well as the solutions to the problem of cognition in the first part of this work, irresistibly imply to a new metaphysics and with it a sketch to a new theory of truth. This will be my secondary goal into which I will delve deeper into the second part of this chapter.

3.1 Truth is an identity relation

First of all, there is a theory that directly confirms the thesis presented here, and that is the identity theory of truth: "The simplest and most general statement of the identity theory of truth is that when a truth-bearer (e.g., a proposition) *is true*, there is a truth-maker (e.g., a fact) with which it is identical and the truth of the former *consists in* its identity with the latter" (Candlish, Damnjanovic, entry). Elsewhere it reads that the identity theory "...has often been treated as the theory that true propositions and facts are identical (and that this identity constitutes the nature of truth)" (Candlish, Damnjanovic, para. 3). Roots of this theory can be traced back all the way to the mystical philosophers, such as Plotinus, and it was also espoused by the British philosophers Bertrand Russell and George Edward Moore since 1898 until around 1910.

The main remark and cause for rejection of this theory are that it is absurd to discuss identity between thoughts and reality, that is, between something mental, such as propositions, and something real, such as facts. Supporters of this theory are trying to equate the ontological status of truth-bearers with that of truth-makers through building special types of metaphysics. The attempts at equating go in both directions wherein both types of entities are represented as real beings or as mental beings which would allow for a relation of identity between them – identity either between real or mental entities, but I would say, without much success.[1]

3.2 Correspondence

It is the difference according to the ontological status of truth-bearers and truth-makers that apologists of the theory of correspondence emphasize. It is the most generally accepted theory of truth in modern philosophy. Its modern history dates from the beginning of the 20 century, especially with the works of Russell and Moore in the period after 1910, and its roots can be traced back all the way to Aristotle. Historians of philosophy list Aquinas, Augustine, John Locke, Leibniz, etc. as its proponents. The second main argument in support of thesis presented here can be derived from it.

The modern theory of correspondence occurred as a reaction to the remarks of the identity theory. In a narrower sense, the theory of correspondence is a view according to which the truth is a correspondence of propositions with facts where, unlike the identity theory, the term 'identity' is replaced with the term 'correspondence'. Let us avoid the consider-

---

[1] One such attempt will follow later in this chapter.

able discussion on the great number of versions of the theory with which the analysis presented here will be focused directly on its essence, on what is common to all versions of the theory, and that is the relation of correspondence. It can be immediately noted that there is not a clear definition on the term 'correspondence' – a fact admitted by the very supporters of the theory and this is one of the main remarks directed at it. Through analysis of offered definitions of the term 'correspondence', an attempt will be made to demonstrate that the identity-correspondence replacement is inessential since correspondence is merely a type of identity.

According to one definition "Correspondence holds between a proposition and a fact when the proposition and fact have the same structure, and the same constituents at each structural position. When they correspond, the proposition and fact thus mirror each-other" (Glanzberg, para. 1.1.2). Phrases used here – 'same structure' and 'the same constituents' can be replaced by 'identical structure' and 'identical constituents', respectively, without a change in their meaning. So now the definition of 'correspondence' would be the following: Correspondence holds between a proposition and a fact when the proposition and fact have the identical structure and the identical constituents at each structural position. From this it is clear that correspondence is a type of identity, that is, identity according to the structure.

According to another view, correspondence is an isomorphism (David, para. 6), therefore I will continue with an analysis of the term 'isomorphism'. The word is of Greek origin, and it is coined from the words *isos* meaning 'equal' and *morphē*, meaning 'form'.[2] Today it retained its meaning as similarity in forms, structures, and relations. The similarity can be easily abstracted to identity, which is, in fact, its essence. It can be concluded that isomorphism is a type of identity and if correspondence is an isomorphism, then correspondence is also identity according to form, structure, and relations, which takes us to the same conclusion from above which is another argument in support of the thesis presented here.

In the text of the Austrian philosopher Marian David there is an explicit claim that "The correspondence relation must be some sort of resemblance relation" (David, para. 5), and the term 'resemblance' is but a type of identity.

---

[2] isomorphism. Chambers's Twentieth Century Dictionary. Retrieved December 19, 2015 from <http://www.finedictionary.com/isomorphism.html>.

From all of the above it can be concluded that regardless of the differently defined ontological status of truth-bearers and truth-makers in the theory of correspondence, the truth remains a relation of identity. Defined relations between truth-bearers and truth-makers in the identity theory and correspondence theory act as stronger identity toward weaker, respectively. When I say stronger identity, I mean identity according to more properties. The shortage of properties in the second relation make the ontological properties, that is, the ontological status. In the identity theory, ontological and structural identity is implied, while in the correspondence theory only structural identity is implied. Although the identity is weaker, it is fairly justified for us to speak of correspondence as identity since it is certain that there is no such thing as absolute identity. Identity is a relation, and for a relation to exist there must be at least two things. The very fact that there is a need for two things implies that they are different in at least one thing. Therefore, if one wants to delve deeper, they will even find differences such as the time of occurrence of thoughts of truth-bearers and truth-makers. Similarly, someone can notice that it is absurd to speak of identity when thoughts are different according to the time of occurrence, etc. Between any two things, there can be identity or difference established, it is only a matter of what properties we consider to be relevant. Everything is identical, and everything is different.

In the end, I will use Frege's authority, through one of his citations in which he expresses his dissatisfaction with the correspondence theory: "A correspondence, moreover, can only be perfect if the corresponding things coincide and so **are just not different things** (Emphasis Mine)" (Frege, 1918, 327). When Frege writes of the things that correspond to each other that they 'are just not different things' it is clear that he understands correspondence as an identity because what is not different is simply identical.

Of the analysis of the two more or less dominant modern theories of truth, supported by the mentioned authorities, it can be concluded that the truth is a relation of identity. As such truth is not something that exists in the external reality, it is a mental entity, a name for one of the many types of relations of identity that the reason establishes, a reflection of the reason on itself.

3.3 Sketch of an alternative theory of truth

As it was noted earlier, the main problem with the identity theory was the absurdity of speaking of identity between thoughts and reality, that is, between something mental such as beliefs or propositions and something real as facts. On the other hand, the theory of correspondence which attempts to offer a correction to this flaw in the identity theory is being criticized. Among others, Frege rightfully criticizes the correspondence theory, writing that "It would only be possible to compare an idea with a thing if the thing were an idea too. And then, if the first did correspond perfectly with the second, they would coincide. But this is not at all what people intend when they define truth as the correspondence of an idea with something real. For in this case, it is essential precisely that the reality shall be distinct from the idea. But then there can be no complete correspondence, no complete truth. So nothing at all would be true; for what is only half true is untrue. Truth does not admit of more and less" (Ibid). I am convinced that the complete correspondence Frege speaks of, including the ontological properties between truth-bearers and truth-makers, is possible although he maintains the stance that the truth is indefinable. In that direction, here an attempt will be made to sketch a new metaphysics which will explain truth as a relation of identity between two entities of mental nature. In this regard, I will offer a division of reality as we know it into two kinds which I will call 'independent reality as we know it' and 'dependent reality as we know it'.

3.3.1 Relation between independent reality as we know it and dependent reality as we know it

This new metaphysics is in accordance with and results from the conclusion in the first chapter that everything we know is of mental nature. Namely, it was seen that reason receives signals from the external reality in itself and processes them on the principle of identity and difference and in this way creates mental things as we know them which are in our heads and the totality of which constitutes reality as we know it. If everything we know is of mental nature, then facts and propositions are of mental nature and are in our heads created by reason. How is it then, that we separate them? An attempt will be made here to answer this question through a postulation of two types of reality as we know it, the division of which will be elaborated on the basis of my previous notions on the course of the cognitive process, on arguments by Locke and Hume, as well as on arguments from the modern sense-datum theory.

Let us remind ourselves that earlier, in chapter 1.3, where the processing of the material provided by the senses was the topic of discussion, it was mentioned that this process takes place outside our consciousness and outside the control of our will, automatically. Things such as we know them are a product of reason, but a very important moment is that our free will has got no control over this process. Which and what things will be obtained as a product of the cognitive process depends solely on the type of material provided by the senses and on the principle of its processing, and considering the fact that the principle of its processing is unchangeable, the only remaining dependence is the type of the material provided by the senses. Not just things, also the nature of knowledge based on them are defined solely by the structure of the material provided by the senses, irrespective of our will and this is what we know as facts.

Aside from this cognitive process, we are able, with the power of our reason and with the direction of our will, to freely imagine whatever things we like and create whatever knowledge we like based on them. These creations are what we know as 'propositions'.

Based on this difference I propose the introduction of two new terms which, I will allow myself to call 'independent reality as we know it' and 'dependent reality as we know it'. What will the 'independent reality as we know it' be depends solely on the structure of the material provided by the senses, and with it the nature of the external world or reality in itself, while 'dependent reality as we know it' aside from depending on the nature of the external world, also depends on our will, fantasy, inference, subconsciousness, wishes, or with one word, on everything that constitutes our 'subjectivity'. 'Independent reality as we know it' is the reality created with the processing of material provided by the senses while 'dependent reality as we know it' is created by the additional mediation of our will, imagination, the ability to think, and other factors.

For example, when perceiving my kitchen I notice the table, bills, and other things, and based on them the reason will create the fact that 'the bills are on the table'. Regardless of the number of times, I look away, and no matter how hard I want it, reality will remain unchanged. On the other hand, with the help of my free will, I can create a proposition that for example 'there is a dragon on the table blowing a birthday candle', and it is certain that this is not identical to the knowledge created independently of my free will. If the knowledge is acquired independently of my free will and everything that is implied under 'subjectivity', then it is a fact. If the knowledge is acquired depending on my will and 'subjectivity', then it is a proposition. Facts are truth-makers, while propositions are truth-bearers; the relation of identity between them is truth, and vice versa, the relation of difference is a lie.

Roots of this new distinction can be found in Locke, Hume, and other modern philosophers whose contemplations I will use for its justification and fondness.

Locke's Argument

First and foremost, I will use John Locke's view on the character of our immediate sensory experience as an argument for the justification of this distinction. Locke describes the uniqueness of the nature of the sensory experience with the aim to prove that things exist outside of us and independently of our existence. He lists a few properties that separate ideas which are the result of the sensory experience from ideas which are the result of our imagination or memory. The independence of our experience from our will is the first property he emphasizes, saying that "...there is a manifest difference between the ideas laid up in my memory (over which, if they were there only, I should constantly have the same power to dispose of them, and lay them by at pleasure) and those which force themselves upon me, and I cannot avoid having" (Locke, 1689, book IV, chap. 11, para. 5). Further Locke notes that "...our senses assist one another's testimony of the existence of outward things, and enable us to predict" (op. cit., para. 7), as well as that "pleasure or pain, which accompanies actual sensation, accompanies not the returning of those ideas without the external objects" (op. cit., para. 6).

The American philosopher Laurence BonJour excellently sums up Locke's description of the sensory experience in two properties: "(i) its involuntary character, i.e., the fact that it simply occurs with no choice or control on the part of the person having the experience; (ii) the systematic order or coherence of that experience" (BonJour, para. 2.2). The systematic order will come to the fore when, for example, we are reading a book over and over, and the long series of letters will each time have the same order which is impossible to hold in our memory or to be created in our imagination. Additionally, the same order will exist for every other reader which is an overlap assuming that the book is a product of our imagination, that is, our freely created reality as we know it, completely impossible.

Locke actually describes (what I call here) 'independent reality as we know it', while beside the independence of our will he lists another, striking difference between it and the 'dependent reality as we know it', and that is the systematic order or coherence. It is simply impossible for our free-willed thoughts to flow so coherently and systematically with identical internal pattern and predictability as to mirror the pattern and systematics of our perception.³

Hume's Argument

My distinction between the 'dependent' and the 'independent reality as we know it' greatly corresponds with Hume's distinction between impressions and ideas. Here is how Hume begins the 'Of the Origin of Our Ideas' chapter:

> All the perceptions of the human mind resolve themselves into two distinct kinds, which I shall call IMPRESSIONS and IDEAS. The difference betwixt these consists in the degrees of force and liveliness, with which they strike upon the mind, and make their way into our thought or consciousness. Those perceptions, which enter with most force and violence, we may name impressions; and under this name, I comprehend all our sensations, passions and emotions, as they make their first appearance in the soul. By ideas I mean the faint images of these in thinking and reasoning; such as, for instance, are all the perceptions excited by the present discourse, excepting only, those which arise from the sight and touch, and excepting the immediate pleasure or uneasiness it may occasion. I believe it will not be very necessary to employ many words in explaining this distinction. (Hume, 1739 - 40, 7)

Hume's impressions actually, according to his description, correspond to the things that constitute the 'independent reality as we know it' while the ideas correspond to the things that constitute the 'dependent reality as we know it'.⁴ I will accept 'force' and 'liveliness' from him as properties according to which it is distinguished between the independent and the dependent reality.

Givenness Criteria Argument

The independent reality as we know it is actually one of which we are directly aware of our sensory experience, the perceptional awareness of the physical objects which is known as 'givenness' in modern epistemol-

---

³ Also, in the paper by Laurence BonJour in 'The Representative Realist Explanation of Experience' section there is an outstanding elaboration on the meaning of these properties with few more specific points which could be used here as a description of the 'dependent reality as we know it' without any alterations.

⁴ Further in the same chapter Hume argues that ideas, that is, the 'dependent reality as we know it', are created on the basis of the independent, i.e. the impressions through their various combining.

ogy. Hence, the specific properties of the independent reality as we know it which separate it from the dependent reality as we know it, are actually the criteria of the givenness of a sensible thing.

One of the standard criteria relates to the idea of inference: "something is immediately experienced or is given if the cognitive consciousness of it is not arrived at via any sort of inferential process" (BonJour, para. 1.1). As it was shown earlier, the process of inference of the reason is nothing but identification and differentiation, and it is present from the very beginning of the cognitive process – as early as the creation of elementary sensations which develop rapidly and of which we are not aware and all the way to the highest conscious forms of cognition. Hence, I will question this criterion of distinction between the dependent and the independent reality as we know it (and even for determining givenness). There seems to be a need to specify the term 'inference', therefore, certain more complex and slower processes of inference in which our consciousness – that is, subjectivity as a factor – comes into play, can be the criteria while the point of transition of the quantity into a complexity of a new property remains unclear.

Another criterion which relates to the idea of certainty according to which givenness is determined: "something is immediately experienced or given if the awareness of it is incapable of being mistaken" (BonJour, para. 1.1). I consider this 'incapable of being mistaken' to be a property that excellently describes the knowledge created independently of our will and subjectivity and with that an excellent criterion for distinguishing between propositions and facts. Still, there are certain justified remarks against this criterion considering the fact that, at least in theory, each perceptional experience is subject to mistakes, as can be concluded based on the existence of illusions, hallucinations, etc.

The contemporary English philosopher Tim Crane, analyzing the difference between the nature of experience and the nature of our beliefs writes that "Perception seems to involve a particular kind of "presence to the mind"" (Crane, para. 2.1.2). He further determines the meaning of this specific presence in the mind thus:

> So what is this perceptual presence? Consider again the difference between perception and pure thought (i.e., thought which is non-perceptual). The idea that the objects of perception actually are mind-independent does not distinguish perception from pure thought, since in thinking about the mind-independent world my thought too presents mind-independent objects. Thought, like perception, goes straight out to the world itself. But a difference

between them is that in the case of thought, how the actual object of thought is at the moment I am thinking of it does not in any way constrain my thinking of it; but in the case of perception it does. My perception of the churchyard is immediately responsive to how the churchyard is now, as I am perceiving it. But my (non-perceptual) thought need not be: in the middle of winter, I can imagine the churchyard as it is in spring, I can consider it covered in autumn leaves, and I can think of it in all sorts of ways which are not the ways it presently is. I can think of all these things in their absence. This is not available in perception, because perception can only confront what is presently given: in this sense, it seems that you can only see or hear or touch what is there. It is because of this that perception is sometimes said to have an immediacy or vividness which thought lacks. (Crane, para. 2.1.2)

'The difference between perception and pure thought' as a difference between two mental realities, of which Crane speaks, is actually the difference between the independent and dependent reality as we know it which I want to describe, which is a wonderful overlap. From him, I will accept and use the properties of 'immediacy' and 'vividness' (which overlaps with Hume's 'liveliness') as specific properties of the independent reality as we know it.

It can be concluded that Locke, Hume, Crane, and the remaining mentioned thinkers, although not obviously at first glance and using different terminology, actually speak on the same topic. There are justified remarks on some of the mentioned criteria, but in addition, if not completely, we can conclude that at last partially they found the difference between these two types of realities as we know them and with that the difference between propositions and facts. In the following philosophical investigations, the exact determination of givenness will be the exact determination of the independent reality as we know it.

On Objectivity as a Universal Consent

Despite this, maybe the most striking property distinguishing between and defining both realities, which results as an effect of the involuntary character of the independent reality as we know it is 'objectivity' which will now be elaborated.

Berkeley has brilliantly concluded that we cannot be just like that naively certain that our reality is real and objective, and not an illusion, created by our mind; and raised the question of objectivity which is usually taken for granted. Commonsense, naïve obviousness for the objectivity of our reality is based solely on the consent of cognitive subjects. Here is where this consent comes from: each subject of cognition independently builds a reality for itself, but this does not mean that these separate realities that we perceive will be different. Namely, they are not different because the cognitive reason has neither freedom nor independent will while building the reality in itself. Each subject of cognition creates the independent reality as we know it independently of the subjective will and automatically, with the processing of the same reality in itself, with the same senses, using the same principle; hence, although created separately, our independent realities are common, same to all cognitive subjects. As a matter of fact, this consent, as a type of 'common illusion' is the only criterion for the objectivity of knowledge such as we are naively aware of, and which is in fact only a seeming objectivity. The independent reality as we know it is necessarily identical to all cognitive subjects as opposed to the dependent reality as we know it which is different for each subject of cognition. Her elements may be but are not necessarily identical to the remaining cognitive subjects.

Illusions and Hallucinations

The illusion is to be understood as applying to "... any perceptual situation in which a physical object is actually perceived, but in which that object perceptually appears other than it really is. For example, a white wall in yellow light can look yellow; and sweet drink can taste sour if one has just eaten something sweeter; a quiet sound can sound loud if it is very close to you; and so on" (Crane, para 1.2). Hallucination, on the other hand, "... is an experience that seems like a perception of a real, mind-independent object, but where there is no mind-independent object of the relevant kind being perceived" (Crane, para 1.3). Hallucinations can be caused by mental illness, the use of certain drugs or alcohol, etc.

Both phenomena represent the corruption of the independent reality as we know it. However, I think that the key difference between these two phenomena is that illusions are common to all subjects, so to each subject the white wall will look yellow in the yellow light, to each subject the sweet drink will taste sour if they ate something sweeter, and so on. Conversely, hallucinations are purely subjective and individual.

This difference leads us to the conclusion that one type of corruption comes from "outside" and the other comes "from within". The illusions stem from the objective reality as we know it, as a consequence of the imperfection of our cognitive apparatus. On the other hand, hallucinations or, for example, the thoughts of people who suffer from schizophrenia, stem from the dependent reality as we know it. In hallucinations, certain images or thoughts arising from our subjectivity, in a way, represent us as part of the independent reality as we know it. The illusions are common to all subjects, and the hallucinations are purely subjective and individual because the objective reality is the same for all while the dependent reality as we know it is individual. The phenomena of illusions and hallucinations are another argument in favor of the correctness of the division of reality as we know it into independent and dependent.

3.3.2 Three types of truth

I consider all of the criteria mentioned until now to be sufficient to accept the existence of two types of reality as we know it – and these are the reality which the mind creates automatically and independently of our will, that depends solely on the material provided by the senses; and another reality that is created depending on our will and other subjective factors. Based on this new metaphysics truth can be defined as a relation of identity between the belief from the dependent and from the independent reality as we know it. At the same time, the criterion for the truth is the independent reality as we know it which is in fact what seems to us or what we naively and realistically know as objective reality.

This is, however, just one type of truth, the most common meaning of the term, but not the only type. Truth defined thus, as a relation between two mental entities, does not mean that it has no relation to the external material world which is the object of our cognition. Quite the contrary, independent reality as we know it is directly related to the material reality in itself. As it was concluded earlier while analyzing the faculty of sensibility – there is an identity-difference mirroring of the material into mental, i.e. there is an identity between the identity-difference structures of reality in itself and reality as we know it.[5] Let me further specify this proposition by saying that this identity exists between the reality in itself and the independent reality as we know it. It can be said that this is the second type of truth understood, as it was seen earlier, as an identity according to the structure. The most suitable term for this type of truth is correspondence. It can be said that this is a 'weak' type of truth since it is a relation of identity only according to one abstract property between mental and material entities, and this is the identity-difference structure. The criterion for this type of truth is a reality in itself, and it can be cor-

---

[5] See chapter 1.3.4 (Problem of Justification).

rupted by the imperfections in our cognitive apparatus, such as illusions, flaws and maladies of the sensory organs or the reason, etc.

Despite this, it can be said that there is a third type of truth which is a relation of identity between entities from the dependent reality as we know it. Let us consider the proposition that we tell our psychiatrist 'I dreamt of a dragon blowing birthday candle' or the proposition 'I decided to quit my job yesterday'. Neither one of these propositions nor the authentic dream and the authentic act of deciding do correspond to anything in our sensory experience or anything in the material reality in itself, and yet they are indisputably true. This type of truth is a relation of identity between entities inside the freely created reality as we know it with influence on the free will and other subjective factors. The criterion for this type of truth would be the entity from the dependent reality as we know it which chronologically precedes.

4.

Reason as an aesthetical subject – beauty

To Kurt Cobain

"Beauty is truth, truth beauty,"—that is all
Ye know on earth, and all ye need to know. – John Keats

One of the most striking appearances of the reason is its role of a beholder and creator of beauty. Beauty is a fascinating and controversial riddle occupying minds of philosophers since Antiquity. It is the central notion of aesthetics and one of three ultimate philosophical values, along with the goodness and the truth. Therefore, a work aiming to explain the principle on which the reason functions would be incomplete without investigating beauty.

The primary goal of this work is to answer the fundamental metaphysical question – What is beauty? The first part of this chapter will be dedicated to solving this problem where an attempt will be made to defend the thesis that beauty is the specific relation of identity and that when the reason cognizes beauty, it actually identifies, that is, cognizes a relation of identity. Two types of arguments will serve this purpose. The first type comes from the existing theories of the history of philosophy, and above all, the classic theory of beauty will be used as a foundation. The other type of arguments comes from the analysis of aesthetical categories.

The second part of this chapter will be dedicated to a secondary goal – the ontological aspect of the problem of beauty which relates to its objective or subjective nature. The solution to this problem which will be offered is based on the definition of beauty as a relation of identity, as well as on the new metaphysics which was presented in the previous chapter.

4.1 Classical theory of beauty

The classical philosophical concept of beauty stems from the study of the Western classical and neoclassical architecture, poetry, painting, sculpture, music, and literature. As the American philosopher, Crispin Sartwell writes: "The classical conception is that beauty consists of an arrangement of integral parts into a coherent whole, according to proportion, harmony, symmetry, and similar notions" (Sartwell, para. 2.1). Its roots can be found in Aristotle according to whom "The chief forms of beauty are order and symmetry and definiteness, which the mathematical sciences demonstrate in a special degree" (Metaphysics, XIII, 3, 1078b11-13). In the Ancient Roman architect Vitruvius there is a less abstract classical definition of beauty in architecture: "Architecture depends on Order (in Greek τάξις), Arrangement (in Greek διάθεσις), Eurythmy, Symmetry, Propriety, and Economy (in Greek οικονομία)" (Vitruvius, book I, chap. II, 1). Analyzing Italian painting and architecture, the Swiss art historian Heinrich Wölfflin summarized precisely the classical conception of beauty: "The central idea of the Italian Renaissance is that of perfect proportion. In the human figure as in the edifice, this epoch strove to achieve the image of perfection at rest within itself. Every form developed to self-existent being, the whole freely co-ordinated: nothing but independently living parts" (Wölfflin, 1932, 9–10).

Philosophy knows of other theories of beauty. Kant, for example, defines beauty as disinterest pleasure, which creates a contrast between the aesthetical and the practical. On the other hand, many philosophers have gone in the opposite direction and have identified beauty with suitedness to use.[1] I would say that the connection between the suitedness to use and beauty is far from essential; the aesthetic and the practical are not true contrasts. Namely, the useful can be beautiful and ugly, and the beautiful can be useful and harmful. This is why it is not at all uncommon for opposite interpretations to be equally plausible.

I would also disagree that the classical theory completely and essentially explains the true nature of beauty[2] and I would disagree that beauty is exhausted with the categories of symmetry and proportion. In this respect, Plotinus, which is considered as one of the representatives of the idealistic theory of beauty, criticizes symmetry, and with that, the classical conception of beauty. His critique is based on the fact that there are beautiful things that bear no relation to symmetry, and similarly there are symmetrical things that are still not beautiful: "Again since the one face, constant in symmetry, appears sometimes fair and sometimes not, can we doubt that beauty is something more than symmetry, that symmetry itself owes its beauty to a remoter principle?" (First Ennead, Sixth Tractate, Beauty, 1). Plotinus does not com-

---

1 See Crispin Sartwell, "Beauty", The Stanford Encyclopedia of Philosophy, chapter 2.5.
2 More on this issue in chapter 4.4.2.

pletely reject symmetry considering the fact that he admits that symmetry contains beauty, he only claims that beauty is due to a remoter principle. I consider this critique to be completely justified. Further, in search of this principle, he claims that: „....all the loveliness of this world comes by communion in Ideal-Form" (First Ennead, Sixth Tractate, Beauty, 2) and, quite vaguely, concludes that „...material thing becomes beautiful- by communicating in the thought that flows from the Divine." (First Ennead, Sixth Tractate, Beauty, 2). However, regardless of this vagueness, Plotinus was definitely onto something. In the following pages through analysis of symmetry and other principles which are known to contain beauty, I will try to determine this remoter principle.

What is notable in these classical definitions is that, despite the others, the use of two terms with the aim to define beauty is repeated over and over again. These two terms are symmetry and proportion. They will be analyzed in more depth, and an attempt will be made to show that they are in their essence types of identity relations.

The fact that symmetry is a type of identity relation can be easily established through analysis of its definition: symmetry is "The quality of being made up of exactly similar parts facing each other or around an axis."[3] According to this, one can say that symmetry is essentially an identity relation between two sides or halves of the same object according to size, shape, and position. The same applies to the other meanings of the term 'symmetry'.

Proportion, on the other hand, is also a specific relation of identity, but its reduction is a bit more complicated. Namely, the proportion cannot be reduced to a simple identity relation between the elements, since it is the relation of identity between relations. By definition, the proportion is "The relationship of one thing to another in terms of quantity, size, or number; ratio."[4] For the purpose of this work, it could be defined as a relation between the elements that constitute the aesthetical object. It should be instantly noted that in each complex object, regardless of us describing it as beautiful or ugly, there are relations, that is, proportions between its elements. That is why there is a need to specify that when the classical theory claims that beauty is founded on a proportion it does not mean any proportion, but the relation of identity between proportions in which the first of the four terms divided by the second equals the third divided by the fourth as in $6/3=12/6$.

---

[3] "symmetry, n." *OED Online*, Oxford University Press, June 2017, https://en.oxforddictionaries.com/definition/symmetry. Accessed 29 November 2017.

[4] "proportion, n." *OED Online*, Oxford University Press, June 2017, https://en.oxforddictionaries.com/definition/proportion. Accessed 3 December 2017.

Identity as the essence of proportion is demonstrated best in the so-called 'golden ratio' (golden section).[5] 'Golden section' is by definition "The division of a line so that the whole is to the greater part as that part is to the smaller part (i.e. in a ratio of 1 to 1/2 ($\sqrt{5} + 1$)), a proportion which is considered to be particularly pleasing to the eye."[6] As it can be seen from the definition itself, the golden ratio represents a relation of identity between the ratio of the whole to the larger part and the ratio of the larger part to the smaller. Therefore, although dimensions of elements which are in 'golden ratio' are different, it still evokes a feeling of beauty exactly because of this identity relation. The golden ratio is not a simple relation of identity between elements, but a relation of identity between relations, on a metalevel. This important moment will be emphasized here: The existence of beauty in the golden ratio is a proof that the reason possesses a fascinating ability for the unconscious, automatic identification on a metalevel, and maybe even meta-metalevel, which should be investigated additionally.

I consider the uniqueness of the golden ratio relating to other ratios to be due to the fact that meta-identity in the golden ratio is achieved with a minimal number of different elements, only three, while other attuned and balanced ratios require four elements. Four elements, as opposed to three, implies that in the other proportions there is a greater number of different relations which diminish beauty.

It can be concluded that proportion and symmetry are types of identity relations and when Classicists claim beauty to be founded on proportion and symmetry, they actually claim that beauty is based on identity. If the beautiful things are not symmetrical and proportional, as is the case with many

---

[5] It is considered esthetically attractive proportion. It is known under different names, such as 'extreme and mean ratio', 'divine proportion', 'divine section', 'golden cut', 'golden number', etc. The great mathematician and astronomer Johannes Kepler describes golden ratio as 'precious jewel'. The astrophysicist Mario Livio dedicates an entire work to proportion, where he says: "Some of the greatest mathematical minds of all ages, from Pythagoras and Euclid in ancient Greece, through the medieval Italian mathematician Leonardo of Pisa and the Renaissance astronomer Johannes Kepler, to present-day scientific figures such as Oxford physicist Roger Penrose, have spent endless hours over this simple ratio and its properties. But the fascination with the Golden Ratio is not confined just to mathematicians. Biologists, artists, musicians, historians, architects, psychologists, and even mystics have pondered and debated the basis of its ubiquity and appeal. In fact, it is probably fair to say that the Golden Ratio has inspired thinkers of all disciplines like no other number in the history of mathematics" (Livio, 2002, 6).

[6] "golden section, n." *OED Online*, Oxford University Press, June 2017, https://en.oxforddictionaries.com/definition/golden_section. Accessed 3 December 2017.

pieces of modern art, then their beauty lies in another type of identity. Further, we will discuss these other types of identity.

4.2 Analysis of aesthetical categories

The quest for the Holy Grail of esthetics has still not ended. There still is no universal recipe, a divine methodology for creating beauty, but I would say that its fragments are known in theory, and their application results in the creation of a certain beauty. Additionally, some of these fragmented recipes shall be analyzed with the aim to locate the common in all of them which will unite them in a sole universal principle for the creation of beauty.

Symmetry or proportion are such fragments of the universal recipe, and it is clear that their application in the creation of a certain structure will result in a certain beauty if not more, at least in relation to another structure where there is a completely chaotic combination of elements from which it is made of. Additionally, it will be concluded that beside symmetry and proportion, all other aesthetical categories that contain beauty, are essentially names for different types of identity relations. First and foremost, I will look into the so-called figures of speech which are used in rhetoric, poetry, and literature. After that, I will look into musical, and other aesthetical categories whose use in art is known to evoke certain beauty:

- **Metaphor**: „…the most important and widespread figure of speech, in which one thing, idea, or action is referred to by a word or expression normally denoting another thing, idea, or action, so as to suggest some common quality shared by the two. In metaphor, this resemblance is assumed as an imaginary identity rather than directly stated as a comparison: referring to a man as that pig, or saying he is a pig is metaphorical…" (Baldick, 2001, 153). In this definition of metaphor, it is clearly stated that the replacement of a word or expression with another word or expression is based on the certain identity between them. The richer in content the identity relation, the more beautiful the metaphor.

- **Anaphora**: „…a rhetorical figure of repetition in which the same word or phrase is repeated in (and usually at the beginning of) successive lines, clauses, or sentences. Found very often in both verse and prose, it was a device favoured by Dickens and frequently used in the free verse of Walt Whitman. These lines by Emily Dickinson illustrate the device:

> Mine—by the Right of the White Election!
> Mine—by the Royal Seal!
> Mine—by the Sign in the Scarlet prison
> Bars—cannot conceal!" (Baldick, 2001, 11).

The concept of repetition contains in itself identity, and according to this, it can be said that the anaphora is a relation of identity according to the initial phrase or word in successive lines, clauses, or sentences.

- **Epistrophe**: „...a rhetorical figure by which the same word or phrase is repeated at the end of successive clauses, sentences, or lines, as in Whitman's Song of Myself (1855):

> The moth and the fish-eggs are in their place,
> The bright suns I see, and the dark suns I cannot see are in their place,
> The palpable is in its place, and the impalpable is in its place" (op. cit., 85).

Or, epistrophe is a relation of identity according to the final expression or word in successive phrases, clauses, sentences, or verses.

- **Alliteration**: "...(also known as 'head rhyme' or 'initial rhyme'), the repetition of the same sounds—usually initial consonants of words or of stressed syllables—in any sequence of neighbouring words: 'Landscapelover, lord of language' (Tennyson)" (op. cit., 6). Or, alliteration is a relation of identity according to the initial consonants between two or more neighboring words or syllables.

- **Rhyme**: "...the identity of sound between syllables or paired groups of syllables, usually at the ends of verse lines" (op. cit., 218).

- **Meter**: "...the pattern of measured sound-units recurring more or less regularly in lines of verse" (op. cit., 154). This pattern of measured sound-units essentially consists of creation of two types of identities in verses: (1) relation of identity between feet according to their structure; and (2) relation of identity between verses according to the number of feet (and syllables at the same time) they have, where 'foot' is "...a group of syllables taken as a unit of poetic metre in traditional prosody, regardless of word boundaries. As applied to English verse, the foot is a certain fixed combination of syllables, each of which is counted as being either stressed (') or unstressed (x);" (op. cit., 99). In the Western theory of poetry there is a difference between qualitative and quantitative meter. In the qualitative meter the structure of the foot consists of a combination of accented and nonaccented syllables. The structure of the foot in the quantitative meter consists of a combination of longer and shorter syllables. In certain languages where there is no accent and where the differences according to the lengths of syllables are minimal, the meter is merely an identity according to the number of syllables. Since the structure implies arrangement of relations between certain elements, in this case - syllables, and meter is the relation of identity between structures, it can be said that meter is a metarelation of identity or relation between relations, similar to the golden section.

- **Assonance**: "…the repetition of identical or similar vowel sounds in the stressed syllables (and sometimes in the following unstressed syllables) of neighbouring words; it is distinct from rhyme in that the consonants differ although the vowels or diphthongs match: sweet dreams, hit or miss" (op. cit., 20). Or, assonance is the relation of identity according to the vowels between neighboring words.

- **Consonance**: "the repetition of identical or similar consonants in neighbouring words whose vowel sounds are different (e.g. coming home, hotfoot)" (op. cit., 49). Or, consonance is a relation of identity according to the consonants between neighbouring words.

- **Anadiplosis**: "…a rhetorical figure of repetition in which a word or phrase appears both at the end of one clause, sentence, or stanza, and at the beginning of the next, thus linking the two units, as in the final line of Shakespeare's 36th sonnet: As thou being mine, mine is thy good report" (op. cit., 9). Or, anadiplosis is a relation of identity between the last and the first word or phrase of two neighboring clauses, sentences, or stanzas.

- **Epanalepsis**: "…a figure of speech in which the initial word of a sentence or verse line reappears at the end" (op. cit., 81), as in 'Only the poor really know what it is to suffer; only the poor'. Or, epanalepsis is a relation of identity between a word used at the beginning and the end of a sentence or verse line.

- **Metonymy**: "…a figure of speech that replaces the name of one thing with the name of something else closely associated with it, e.g. the bottle for alcoholic drink, the press for journalism, skirt for woman, Mozart for Mozart's music, the Oval Office for the US presidency" (op. cit., 154). Here the relation of identity is not so obvious. Metonymy, in a certain sense, as it can be seen from the definition, implies replacement of names based on the association unlike metaphor where names are replaced based on identity according to a property. However, it was demonstrated previously that association too is a specific type of identification,[7] and it can be concluded accordingly that metonymy as a result of identification, is a type of relation of identity. The same applies if metonymy is understood as a replacement of something with its attribute. In the *Deduction*[8] chapter it was demonstrated that there is an identity between the thing and the quality or the attribute that belongs to it, which can be best portrayed as in identity between a sub-

---

[7] See chapter 2.5.
[8] See chapter 2.2.

set and a set. Therefore, the replacement of names which metonymy implies is a replacement on the basis of identity.

- **Onomatopoeia:** "…the use of words that seem to imitate the sounds they refer to (whack, fizz, crackle, hiss); or any combination of words in which the sound gives the impression of echoing the sense" (op. cit., 178). Imitation implies a relation of identity between what is being imitated and the result of the imitation. According to this, onomatopoeia is a relation of identity between a word and a natural sound.

- **Parallelism:** "…the arrangement of similarly constructed clauses, sentences, or verse lines in a pairing or other sequence suggesting some correspondence between them. The effect of parallelism is usually one of balanced arrangement achieved through repetition of the same syntactic forms" (op. cit., 183), as 'The bigger they are, the harder they fall'. Or, parallelism is a relation of identity according to the syntactic forms of two or more clauses sentences, or verse lines.

- **Antimetabole**: "…a figure of speech in which a pair of words is repeated in reverse order: 'All for one, and one for all'" (op. cit., 13). As it can be noticed, the pair of words are symmetrical, and symmetry, as was demonstrated above, is just one type of identity.

- **Simile:** "…an explicit comparison between two different things, actions, or feelings, using the words 'as' or 'like', as in Wordsworth's line: I wandered lonely as a cloud" (op. cit., 237). The words 'as' or 'like' actually denote identity according to a certain property.

- **Polysyndeton** "…a rhetorical term for the repeated use of conjunctions to link together a succession of words, clauses, or sentences, as in Keats's Endymion (1818):

And soon it lightly dipped, and rose, and sank,

And dipped again …" (op. cit., 199).

Or, Polysyndeton is a relation of identity according to conjunctions between consecutive words, clauses, or sentences.

Music is defined as an organized sound with rhythm and harmony as its fundamental elements. It is indisputable that the combination of sounds that have rhythm and harmony has an esthetic value – beauty, as opposed to the combination of sounds not having these elements. It can be said that exactly rhythm and harmony give the sound its organization to become music. As it will be shown further, these two categories essentially are types of identity relations.

- **Rhythm** is by definition "a strong, regular repeated pattern of movement or sound. 2. The systematic arrangement of musical sounds, principally according to duration and periodical stress."[9] Repetition itself implies a relation of identity between repeating elements. Or, essentially, the musical rhythm is a relation of the identity of time intervals, regardless of whether the intervals have been determined by rests, beats, notes, groups (patterns) of beats or notes, etc.

- **Harmony**

Musical harmony is by definition "the combination of simultaneously sounded musical notes to produce a pleasing effect."[10] Pythagoras noticed that instrument strings produce harmonious tones when the coefficients of their lengths are whole numbers. Modern research in physics confirms this revelation and shows that harmonic frequencies are all multiples of the same fundamental frequency. For example, notes at frequencies of 200, 300, and 400 Hertz are all multiples of 100.[11] In physics, it is known that waves with different frequencies combine when travelling through the same medium, and the resulting wave of this combination will have a regular structure which will be periodically repeated only if the frequencies are all multiples of the same fundamental frequency.[12] The regularity and repetition of the resulting waves mean that its form and the moments when its amplitude reaches minimum and maximum values are regular and periodical. Each structure possessing regularity and repetition in itself contains identities, and harmony specifically can be understood as a super swift micro rhythm where the minimum and maximum values of the amplitudes play the role of beats. Perception of these identities is the cause for the beauty we experience in harmony. Otherwise, the resulting wave will be irregular and unpleasant to our ear.

In theory of music, it is known that there is another way of combining sounds that results in a pleasant feeling or beauty, and that is combining of sounds with very similar frequency and is known as a beat phenomenon. When waves with very similar frequency are combined, a wave is obtained as a result possessing periodicity and regularity which are manifested as peri-

---

[9] "rhythm, n." *OED Online*, Oxford University Press, June 2017, https://en.oxforddictionaries.com/definition/rhythm. Accessed 29 November 2017.

[10] "harmony, n." *OED Online*, Oxford University Press, June 2017, https://en.oxforddictionaries.com/definition/harmony. Accessed 29 November 2017.

[11] For a more detailed explanation go to: <http://www.physicsclassroom.com/class/sound/Lesson-4/Fundamental-Frequency-and-Harmonics>.

[12] For a more detailed explanation go to: <http://www.physicsclassroom.com/Class/sound/u11l3a.cfm#music>.

odical and regular shifts between soft and loud sounds. Hence, the combination of sound waves with very similar frequency will be pleasant to our ear thanks to the identity which is contained in these regular repetitions.[13]

It can be concluded that beauty coming from harmony in music is based on relations of identity in the internal structure of the sound waves which are a result of the interference.

****

As it can be noted, common to proportion and symmetry with which classicists define beauty, as to the plentitude of other aesthetical concepts in which beauty is contained, is that these are all types of identity relations. It is certain that beauty is not exhausted by these categories, however, I consider them to be sufficient to lead us to an inductive conclusion: based on these notions one unique and universal aesthetical principle can be identified – definition of beauty which can be applied to all aesthetical objects and that is that beauty, in general, is an identity relation.

Perception of identity relations is what causes the pleasant feeling we call beauty. Appropriately, ugliness is a relation of difference. When an object in its structure possesses any of these aesthetical categories as its properties, this means that this object possesses relations of identity, and with that, beauty. All other beauty not encompassed with these concepts consists of relations of identity which are still not generally agreed upon or which are unique, and according to this, they cannot be categorized. Beauty is not present only in artistic works, but everywhere where identity relations are present. Every time the reason makes an analogy, it adopts an inductive or deductive conclusion, analyses or synthesizes, solves mathematical or logical problems, generalizes, does good deeds or loves[14] it experiences the beauty of the same kind as when it contemplates any art. Once you feel beauty start searching for the identity right away, be sure it is there.

These conclusions can be supported by the authority of Francis Hutcheson, Scottish philosopher from the 18 century, who shares the views presented here: "The Figures which excite in us the Ideas of Beauty, seem to be those in which there is Uniformity amidst Variety" (Hutcheson, 1726, Treatise I, sec. II, para. III). Hutcheson goes a step further from the rest of the theoreticians of classical beauty by making the proper generalization using the right terms – 'uniformity' and 'variety' – because of uniformity in general, as a

---

[13] It is interesting to note the ability of reason to identify between so small segments on an unconscious level.

[14] Love and goodness as identities will be covered in the next chapter.

quality to a certain structure, results only from the relations of identity between the elements of this structure. Similar ideas can be found in the English poet Coleridge in his *On Poesy or Art* essay where he philosophically discusses the essence of beauty. He writes: "And what then is beautiful? What is beauty? It is, in the abstract, the unity of the manifold, the coalescence of the diverse." Later to confirm that "...pleasure consists in the identity of two opposite elements, that is to say, – sameness and variety. ...This unity in multeity I have elsewhere stated as the principle of beauty" (Coleridge, 1836, Lecture XIII).

It can be concluded that beauty is a relation of identity which is a result of identification and differentiation as operations of reason or, in other words, beauty is one of the manifestations of the principle of identity and difference.

4.3 Enslaving of the muses

Now, if one presumes that they know what the essence of beauty is, does an opportunity arise to 'artificially' create it, instead of depending on the good graces of the muses, as until now? Can beauty be created by a technician, and even machine, which will follow certain rules and procedures, and not as until now be a result of the moment of inspiration of chosen geniuses?

In order to create a beautiful structure, one needs to arrange its elements so there are as much as possible identity relations and as less as possible difference relations between them. This is only apparently a simple task. Creation of identities is a double-edged sword since in order to create any relation, be it a relation of identity, one must incorporate in the structure at least two different entities. Entities used to build the structure possess various modes of comparison. Identity according to only one mode means an unwanted difference according to all other modes. Hence, with each new arbitrarily created relation of identity, the number of differences the structure contains is increased, meaning that its discord is increased, i.e. its ugliness. Aside from this, the possibility of the reason to identify and differentiate on a metalevel between relations themselves is also something to be mentioned and to be taken into consideration in order to obtain the complete picture of the creation of beauty. The artist, consciously or not, searches for identities in the process of creation, and skilled artist is the one able to identify according to a larger number of properties and able to identify according to relations, which is, of course, a much more complicated skill, such that requires a greater power of abstraction.

The most logical first step in the direction of artificial creation of beauty would be the analysis of the already existing aesthetical objects for which there is no doubt, or there is the least doubt in their beauty and complete deconstruction of their identity-difference structure, upon which their imitation would ensue. At the same time, it is necessary to consider that in the rationalization there can lurk danger which threatens to destroy beauty. The development of a mathematical method or software that effectively combines 'uniformity amidst variety' to create the most identities between the least differences will mean death to the artists as we know them. These notions give rise to new opportunities for experimenting in art and creating new, maybe never before seen, forms of beauty because now we know what to look for.

Can beauty be exactly measured? Assuming the thesis that beauty is a relation of identity is correct, then the smallest quantity of beauty would be one identity relation. Measuring being simply the counting of identities and differences contained by the aesthetical object, wherein beauty would be the quotient of the sums of identities and differences or expressed mathematically as $B = \sum rI / \sum rD$, seems too simple to be true. This formula would apply only under the assumption that each elementary identity, and that would be an identity according to only one elementary property, has equal value for us. Does the identity according to one property have the same value as the identity according to another is an open question requiring additional investigation. Many other questions arise here: Which are the elementary properties and what is their relation to the complex modes of comparison? Does the identity between the elements have the same value as the identity between relations? Can one make a complete and exact list of properties, i.e. modes of comparison possessed by elements that comprise the structure of the aesthetical object?

It is certain that the reason performs such 'measuring' of beauty unconsciously and automatically. One could only suppose what a complex task the conscious processing of a melody would be when there would be a need first to determine all simple relations of identity. This would mean to separate and name each individual tone and each rest and determine their properties, that is, measure the heights and the duration of the tones, the duration of the rests, as well as their place in the melody. Then, to consciously compare each one according to each property when we would discover all the simple relations of identity. Then to do the same thing for the relations between relations in order to discover and experience beauty in its entirety. It is clear that reason does all of the above unconsciously. It seems that it is perfectly possible to develop the identity-difference method of analysis theoretically with the help of which the feeling of pleasure or displeasure, beauty or ugliness which presents at the very moment the reason perceives the aesthetical object, will be explained rationally and its origin will be proven, that is, the super swift unconscious processes of identification and differentiation in 'slow motion' will be demonstrated. "Everything beautiful and noble is the result of reason and calculation" (Baudelaire, 1863, 32).

4.4 Ontology of beauty

There are two theoretical approaches in aesthetics that differentiate according to the manner in which they perceive the existence of beauty: objectivistic and subjectivistic. The first considers the beauty to be an objective property of the beautiful things, while the second consider that beauty is subjective – 'in the eye of the beholder'. This is one of the aesthetical problems that attract the most philosophical attention and at the same time the cause for a vast number of disagreements among theoreticians. The definition of beauty proposed in this work, as well as the new metaphysics presented in the previous chapter, allow me to offer one possible answer to this question.

First of all, I consider it necessary to distinguish between the two meanings of subjectivity and objectivity which are not allowed to be mixed. The first, which I will for the needs of this work call 'hard' meaning is the following: Objectivity implies that beauty exists outside our heads as a property of the material things, while subjectivity implies that beauty exists inside our head as a mental entity. The second, which I will for the needs of this work call 'soft' meaning, is objectivity understood as a universal consent as opposed to the subjectivity as individuality. The reasons for this difference will be elaborated.

4.4.1 The 'hard' meaning of distinction

In relation to the so-called 'hard' meaning of distinction, I consider beauty to be purely subjective. This view emerges from the definition of beauty as an identity relation and also from the fact that everything that we know is of a mental nature and is located in our heads. This is the entire epistemological process which takes us to this conclusion: Let us suppose that we experience beauty listening to a certain rhythm. In reality in itself, there is a certain musical instrument on which this melody is played. The information of the rhythm is transmitted through sound waves, unequivocally objective according to their ontological status, that reaches our ear. The ear transforms sound waves into electrical impulses with an identical identity-difference structure. Then the impulses reach the brain where they are processed by reason on the principle of identity and difference, described in the first part: it separates uniformities in themselves that become things as we know them. In this case, those things are beats and silence intervals (rests) which are mental beings, purely subjective according to their ontological status. So far, the process is cognition of things. From here on begins the cognitive process of beauty with which the reason compares beats and silence intervals. After establishing the numerous successive relations of identity, in this case, according to the duration of the beats and rests, the reason experiences that pleasant feeling we call beauty.

In short, the definition of beauty itself as a relation of identity is enough to conclude that it is subjective; for the relations themselves, as entities, exist only in the reason of the subject and not as a property of the beautiful objective things. Beauty is in the reason of the beholder. It is a general name for one of the many types of identity relations that the reason establishes. In the objective reality in itself, there is only potential from which reason is yet to create identities.

4.4.2 The 'soft' meaning of distinction

It is interesting that in certain cases the content of this subjectivity can be common for each subject. The fact that the beauty exists only in the eye of the beholder does not mean that each reason always recognizes different beauty. Therefore, the beauty of the experienced rhythm in the example from above is common to each subject recognizing the rhythm. Each subject that would perceive this rhythm will experience the same beauty because it receives identical sound waves and because everyone's senses and reason, and cognitive apparatus in general, function on the same principle considering our biological identity as human beings and, most importantly, since each reason will process the material provided by the sense organs automatically, regardless of its own free will and its other individual properties. So, in the end, as a result of this processing, each subject will receive an identical number and type of identity relations that actually means identical beauty. On the basis of this consent, the subjects can easily conclude that beauty of the rhythm exists objectively which would be wrong. In this way, we reach the second 'soft' meaning of objectivity as universal consent which is only apparent. The differentiation between the soft and the hard meaning of the subjectivity-objectivity distinction is needed because it is a practice to non-critically suppose that everything for which there exists universal consent has to be objective which is not true. As it was seen before, the universal consent exists among us as subjects according to the independently created realities as we know them which are purely subjective.[15] I consider this erroneous assumption to be the cause for the many disagreements between theoreticians of beauty.

---

[15] See On Objectivity as a Universal Consent section in Chapter 3.3.1.

This universal consent for experienced beauty is possible only when the identity relations in which it is contained are established between the things that belong to the independently created reality as we know it. Two subtypes of this general type of identity relations can be distinguished: The first subtype consists of identity relations between elements that constitute the beautiful object. In painting, these are the relations between colors, shapes, lines, etc. In music, these are the relations between height and duration of tones and rests. In poetry, these are the relations between letters, syllables, and verses, etc. Actually the greatest part of the previously analyzed aesthetical categories, with the exception of metaphor, metonymy, and onomatopoeia, represents an example of this type of identity relations.

The second subtype consists of identity relations between the properties of the beautiful thing and something outside of it in the independently created reality as we know it. It can be another object, a historical event, personality, social or political state, human behavior, or any other context. The portrait, for example, will be beautiful only if the pattern of its lines, shapes, and colors is identical to the pattern of lines, shapes, and colors of the person it portrays, and not only according to the identity of the elements that constitute it. This type of beauty is excellently explained through the esthetic theory of mimesis which is compatible with the theory presented here.[16]

Beauty resulting from the first subtype of relations can be called free, while the one resulting from the second subtype of relations can be called dependent, according to Kant's differentiation between free and dependent beauty which greatly corresponds to the view presented here. Namely, according to Kant "There are two kinds of beauty: free beauty (pulchritudo vaga), or beauty which is merely dependent (pulchritudo adhaerens). The first presupposes no concept of what the object should be; the second does presuppose such a concept and, with it, answering perfection of the object. Those of the first kind are said to be (self-subsisting) beauties of this thing or that thing; the other kind of beauty, being attached to a concept (conditioned beauty), is ascribed to objects which come under the concept of a particular end" (Kant, 1790, part I, § 16, 60).

Nevertheless, there are factors that make this consent between subjects imperfect. Objects which are subject to aesthetical judgment are often too

---

[16] Mimesis is imitation as a relation of the work of art toward reality. According to certain estheticians it is considered the essence of beauty, claim that I do not completely agree with. The essence of imitation consists of an identity relation of the product of imitation with the object being imitated. It is just a special case of identification, one aspect of the universal understanding of beauty as a relation of identity and with that an insufficient general principle to explain all forms of beauty.

complex with a large number of individual elements and a large number of their properties which are in fact modes of comparison. This means that there is a relatively vast number of identity and difference relations inside the work of art if we are talking about free beauty. Not each reason is equally capable of cognizing all identity relations. This is especially true of the metarelations whose cognition requires the greater power of the reason. Further, not every reason is identically directed toward the perception of certain identity relations and not each reason cognizes the same relations at the same moment. The lengthy or repeated perception of some aesthetical object can reveal to us other not yet known identities, that is, other beauty. Thence can result in differences in the aesthetical judgments of different individuals for the same 'softly objective' beauty. When the cognition of a dependent beauty is in question, the differences between subjects can result from not being familiar or not being familiar enough with the context, that is, the thing outside the aesthetical subject it refers to. It is certain that through a more thorough investigation one can recognize other reasons for the differences in the aesthetical judgments between subjects related to this type of beauty; those differences, however, are debatable. It can be concluded that when beauty is contained in identity relations between things from the independent reality as we know it, then it is universal and in this case, there definitely is accounting for taste.

This is not the entire picture. As we all well know, there is no universal consent for each beauty. Beauty for which there is no universal consent is the subjective beauty in the soft meaning of the distinction. It results from identity relations existing between things from the independently created reality as we know it and things from the dependently created reality as we know it.[17] In other words, it results from the identity relations existing between the beautiful thing and the personality of the subject beholding it.

All of us as subjects possess our own dependent reality as we know it with the entities of which we compare the beautiful thing. Dependent reality to us consists of all of our views, beliefs, prejudices, cultural base, social status, education, all of our previous experiences in every sense of the word, emotions, desires, mood, etc. To sum up, everything that constitutes our personality, that makes us who we are. This is a pretty imprecise term, however, I still consider it to be useful. It seems that the psychological term 'personality' corresponds optimally to the unwieldy term 'dependently created reality as we know it'. If we are not entirely sure of their synonymy, then it is certain that the term 'personality' represents a big subset of the term 'dependent reality as we know it' or a type of abstraction of it.

---

[17] For the definitions of these two realities please refer to Chapter 3.3.1.

If there is an identity relation between beliefs, views, emotions reflected by a work of art and the ones possessed by the cognitive subject, then they experience beauty. It will be best to illustrate this with a few examples.

A melancholic subject will find a melancholic song beautiful. A tragic love poem will be beautiful to the subject that had the similar personal experience. If a movie or a picture reflects the political or ideological beliefs and views which are identical to the personal political and ideological views of the subject, then the subject will experience beauty at the moment of perceiving them. These are classic examples of subjective beauty which would not be understandable to the subjects that do not possess the same personal properties and experiences and, consequentially, they cannot identify themselves with the aesthetic object.

The causes for experiencing the beauty of this type can be entirely personal or common for a certain group. When Sartwell claims that "I might enjoy a bittersweet experience before a portrait of my grandmother, for example, or the architecture of a house might remind me of where I grew up" (Sartwell, para.1) it is a typical example of experiencing beauty which is purely subjective in both the soft and the hard meaning of distinction. The architecture of a house can remind the above-mentioned author of the place where he spent his childhood years only if it is identical according to one or more properties to the architecture he was surrounded by in his childhood and which exists as a memory in his experience base. The portrait of his grandmother also stirs the memory and the bittersweet experience only because it is identical to the picture of his grandmother in his memory.

This type of beauty, for example, as well as beauty which consists of identity relations between the properties of the beautiful thing and something outside of it, are not at all the subject of classical theory; it only refers to beauty consisting of identity relations between elements that constitute the beautiful object, which speaks of its incompleteness.

Nevertheless, the aesthetical object is able to communicate with the subject and stir something in it only on the basis of identity. To be touched by art is to be identified with the art. This kind of beauty can be evoked by things which are not works of art at all. Even the most common object identical to the one we know from our childhood, for example, can evoke emotions and beauty in us. Artworks usually strive for universality so they would be able to communicate to as great a number of people as possible.

In spite of the reasons for experiencing beauty being completely personal or completely universal, they can be common only to a certain group of people. As it was seen before, entities belonging to the dependent reality as we know it may or may not be common. Actually there is a large number of common entities between dependently created realities as we know them on more subjects too that, in a similar way as with the consent according to the independent realities as we know them, can give us the apparent feeling of objectivity. For example, for one nation their traditional patriotic songs are beautiful, and a person from a different nation may be completely indifferent to them or consider them not in the least beautiful. What is common to the entire group of subjects is their love for the fatherland which is identical to the love expressed in the mentioned songs. Unrealized love or the state of being in love can also be common to a fairly large number of subjects although as an entity it belongs to the dependent reality as we know it.

Hence, it can be concluded that in the so-called soft meaning of the subjectivity-objectivity distinction, the ontological status of beauty depends on the ontological status of things from whose identity relation it results. The objective approach in esthetics is a result of emphasizing beauty founded on relations between things that belong to the independently created reality as we know it and in this case, there is an accounting for taste. On the other hand, the subjectivist approach in esthetics is a result of the emphasis on beauty founded on relations between things from the independently created reality as we know it and things from the dependently created reality as we know it; in this case, there is no accounting for taste. Most often two general types of relations are present along during each esthetic experience and with that both types of beauty. The woman is beautiful according to the harmony of her proportions and the symmetry of her face and figure which represents objective beauty. She is also beautiful according to the identification of her 'soul' with ours which represents subjective beauty, and she is beautiful as a sexual object which is an example of non-rational beauty. There is much to be investigated and written about the specifics of objective and subjective beauty, but for the purposes of this work the locating and the general definition of sources from which this dual nature results will suffice.[18]

---

[18] Aside from the two general types of relations described here, there is also a third type of relations and with that a third type of beauty between things inside the dependent reality as we know it, analogously to the third type of truth, subject of Chapter 3.3.2. It is, for example, the pleasant feeling felt by the creator of the beauty when in their thoughts they will establish a certain identity relation.

5.
Reason as a moral subject – goodness

> *„...one method will discover to us the Beauty-Good and the Ugliness-Evil." – Plotinus*

Another fundamental form of reason existence is the moral reasoning. The goal of the moral reasoning is to distinguish good from bad and the right from wrong. The goodness is a central category in moral philosophy, and I will make an attempt here to answer the old metaphysical, that is, metaethical question – What is goodness? In order to do this, I will largely rely on the authority of the existing moral theories, above all on moral egalitarianism, according to which equality is the essence of morality. On this foundation, as well as through analysis of a handful of most important ethical categories and principles, I will try to prove that the goodness is, in its essence, a specific identity relation and that the moral reasoning is, in its core, a process of identification and differentiation. In the end, as a logical consequence of these suggested solutions, I will try to ground morality.

5.1 Equality is the essence of morality

This is the fundamental thesis of the so-called moral egalitarianism, which dominates the social, political, and moral philosophy since the end of the 20 century onwards, and its roots date back to antiquity. This thesis will be supported by the authority of moral theoreticians among which is the eminent American philosopher James Griffin who claims that "At the deepest level, there is the requirement of equal respect—to see things morally is to grant everyone some sort of equal standing." (Griffin, 1986, 295). One can freely say that formally, equality exists as an idea in all moral teachings throughout human history, including moral, religious teachings. For example, the Christian concept of morality is based on the view that all men are equal in the eyes of God, that is, that all men are God's children. Equality is one of the principles the French revolution was based upon, and also a part of the preamble of the American Declaration of Independence: "We hold these truths to be self-evident, that all men are created equal...". Today "..."treatment as an equal" is a shared moral standard in contemporary theory..." (Gosepath, para.2.3).

Opponents of egalitarianism, among others, are the so-called rights-based theories of moral. According to these theories the rights established by society are protected and given the highest priority, and consequently, morally acceptable actions are those in accordance with established rights. A serious problem with this type of theory arises when determining which rights should be imposed on citizens, i.e. which rights best reflect human nature and, accordingly, best represent the goals that society strives for. Therefore, when determining these rights, rights theories must rely on a more fundamental moral theory that will determine ethical priorities. In fact, rights by definition are something that applies to all members of society and, therefore, purely formal; they are something in which citizens are equal. Thus, the claim of rights is, in fact, the search for the modes of equality, which should be established in a society. According to this, only fundamental moral egalitarianism might provide a platform for natural human rights.

Utilitarianism: "The creed which accepts as the foundation of morals, Utility, or the Greatest Happiness Principle, holds that actions are right in proportion as they tend to promote happiness, wrong as they tend to produce the reverse of happiness" (Mill, 1843, 9-10), is considered to be another strong opponent of egalitarianism. Aside from John Stuart Mill, other more prominent representatives of classical utilitarianism are Jeremy Bentham, Hobbes, and Hume who is considered a proto-utilitarian. At first glance, this theory appears to be easily refutable given that there are innumerable examples to demonstrate that what benefits us is not at all in accordance with the generally accepted moral beliefs. However, this is not the case.

If, for example, in a situation of five equals with a limited supply of food, an individual appropriates the entire supply, it is undoubtedly beneficial to them, and what is beneficial, according to utilitarians, should be morally correct. However, it is clear that this action is contrary to the just way in which the food should be divided into five equal parts. Mill is aware of the possible conflict between justice and utility and believes that "In all ages of speculation, one of the strongest obstacles to the reception of the doctrine that Utility or Happiness is the criterion of right and wrong, has been drawn from the idea of justice..." (Mill, 1843, 61). The way in which the conflict between utility and justice is resolved is quite interesting: he proclaims justice as the most important of social utilities. Thus the utilitarian can argue that it is morally right to divide the food into five equal parts because such a division is just and justice brings mutual respect and trust that are much more beneficial and offer us much greater happiness than the food would bring us. In this way, there can be no conflict between utility and justice.

Or, we can easily assume a situation where a certain benefit can be gained through lying. If lying is beneficial, is it then morally right? To such an argument, a utilitarian would answer that the act of lying would cause loss of respect and trust, and thus far greater harm to the individual and society than the benefit we could gain by lying. Therefore lying is morally wrong.

In fact, in a similar way, any argument whereby the benefit is opposed to any generally accepted moral belief, utilitarians can solve by extending the meaning of the benefit from the current or the temporary to the long-term and from the individual to the general. In this way, any argument of this type would be made worthless, because it is simply impossible to refute the claim that morality is useful. Thus, if one pushes utilitarians with such arguments, then they will eventually accept every moral belief of egalitarianism and incorporate it into their theory because undoubtedly those beliefs are of inestimable social benefit, i.e. because equal treatment makes us happy and satisfied. According to this, utilitarian moral beliefs will coincide with egalitarian, which, I must admit, is a little ridiculous. The last general conclusion of a utilitarian would be that egalitarianism is a sound theory because it is useful. Accordingly, these two theories are not as contradicting as is commonly believed.

In this sense, one of the consequences of the utilitarian logic is that Mill, for example, advocates equal opportunities for men and women. In doing so, he does not perceive equality as a rational need but only accepts it as useful to society, maximizing human happiness. Also, the utilitarian method implies that everyone's well-being, including one's own, is treated as equally worthwhile. In this regard, isn't Bentham's famous utilitarian axiom "every man to count for one, nobody for more than one" actually an egalitarian thesis?

In essence, it seems that utilitarianism accepts equality as an instrument that is of the highest social utility, and thus tacitly accepts egalitarianism through the back door. In fact, it is impossible for any plausible moral theory to avoid the concept of equality. Ultimately, everything that utilitarianism tells us is that egalitarianism, that is, equality, is beneficial. Then, I would ask, what is the benefit of utilitarianism?

However, while Mill, and utilitarians in general, recognize the existence of equality in moral beliefs, they reject equality as the basis of morality, and this is what essentially differs them from egalitarians. They want to go deeper than equality, accepting utility as the basis of morality. Equality according to them is but an instrument that is valuable only because it plays a causal role in producing pleasure or happiness; pleasure and happiness, however, are "intrinsic" goods, meaning that they are good in themselves and not because they produce some further valuable thing.

The key question that needs to be posed is why exactly actions leading to equality bring us pleasure and happiness, i.e. utility, and the actions leading to inequality cause dissatisfaction and pain? Utilitarianism does not provide a satisfying answer to this question. We must look for the essence of morality, its foundation, elsewhere. The foundation of morality cannot be in its consequence, but in its cause, i.e. in the intrinsic nature of the moral act.

In addition, there are numerous other objections to egalitarianism that I would classify as only seemingly anti-egalitarian. For example, "a sample non-egalitarian would be one who believes that people born into a higher social caste, or a favored race or ethnicity, or with an above-average stock of traits deemed desirable, ought somehow to count for more than others in calculations that determine what morally ought to be done" (Arneson, chap. 1). This opposition to egalitarianism refers to the "equality among whom" debate, not the very principle of equality. The contradiction is therefore insufficient because understood thusly non-egalitarians remain faithful to the "equal for equals" principle.

Or, for example, disagreements arise from the question of what type of equality to apply in a particular situation; is the appropriate type of equality is proportional or numerical? Marx, in this sense, contrary to the proportional equality – according to merit, advocates another form of socio-economic equality: all should be required to contribute to society to the extent of their abilities, and all should be allowed to receive from society in accordance with their needs.

I am convinced that these objections are largely derived from the abstractness and multifaceted concept of equality. "Equality is a contested concept: people who praise it or disparage it disagree about what they are praising or disparaging" (Dworkin, 2000, 2). Morality refers to human relationships, and people are highly complex creatures with many properties and many roles in society which also makes their relations complex and numerous. Therefore, it is no surprise that the answers to these questions are complex and numerous. Although 'treatment as an equal' is a common moral standard practically in all plausible theories of morality, the differences between them show up in the answers of the questions equality of what, equality among whom, equality when and what kind of equality.

Anti-egalitarians are always only against a certain notion of equality. However, regardless of such disagreements, the very principle of equality has never been contested. According to this, it can be said that such contradiction between the moral theories is inessential. Confirmation of such attitudes can be found in the British political theorist David Miller, according to whom "...there are some contemporary political philosophers who would describe themselves as egalitarians, and some who would describe themselves as anti-egalitarians. It may be, as I have argued elsewhere, that this opposition is a false one, and that the debate between so-called egalitarians and so-called anti-egalitarians is better understood as a debate about whether one particular kind of equality – economic equality, say – should be pursued or not." (Miller 1997, [222]). Also, the American philosopher Daniel Hausman generalizes: "...virtually all moral theories find their origin in some notion of equal respect owed to moral agents, and concerns about equality of moral status derive from a concern not about equality itself but rather about a particular kind of status" (Hausman; McPherson, 2006, 195).

****

Relying on the mentioned authorities and arguments, it can be concluded that equality is the foundation of morality and according to this a morally good action is the one resulting in equality between the moral agents. On the other hand, identity is the foundation of equality by which it can be argued that a morally good action is the one resulting in identity between the moral agents, that is, goodness is a relation of identity. As it was previously analyzed, equality is a tripartite relation encompassing a minimum of two things which are objects of comparison, and a minimum of one property according to which they are being compared. The property according to which they are compared is called tertium comparationis, and it is a property that is necessarily owned by both objects of the comparison. If the relation between the two objects is equality, then the relation between the properties of comparison belonging to the two objects is pure identity.

Several abstract modes of comparison will be listed here which are used in contemporary theory and which can be said to be the best generalizations of the numerous concrete modes of comparison. Namely, there can be equality according to resources, quality of life, respect, treatment, fortune, opportunities, human dignity, freedom, equality before the laws, equal human rights, etc. From these substances of equality result in the moral principles which are common to all plausible moral theories today, for example, moral agents are equal according to the treatment provided to them, equal before the law, have equal opportunities, etc.

This types of equalities can be easily reduced to identities in accordance with the above reasoning. Therefore, it can be said that is morally good and right when there is a relation of identity between the quality and the quantity of resources that moral agents have access to. Or, good and right is when there is an identity between the opportunities that various moral agents have at their disposal, identical freedom for all rational beings, etc.

Also, equality has many faces and here are some of them:

This is the definition of formal equality: "When two persons have equal status in at least one normatively relevant respect, they must be treated equally with regard to this respect." (Gosepath, para. 2.1). Aristotle formulates this principle of equality in the following manner: "All men think justice to be a sort of equality, and to a certain extent they agree with what we have said in our philosophical works about ethics. For they say that what is just is just for someone and that it should be equal for equals (Emphasis Mine)" (Politics, III, 12, 1282b16-19). For example, good is if two people that crossed the street in red light receive equal punishments. This relation of identity between the severity of the two punishments is pure goodness. This example can simultaneously serve as an illustration of the manner in which the principle of equality under the law is reduced to pure identity.

Division of equality into proportional and numerical is known since Aristotle. The definition of numerical equality is as follows: "A form of treatment of others or as a result of its distribution is equal numerically when it treats all persons as indistinguishable, thus treating them identically or granting them the same quantity of a good per capita" (Gosepath, para. 2.2). On the other hand, proportional equality is defined thus "a form of treatment of others or distribution is proportional or relatively equal when it treats all relevant persons in relation to their due" (ibid). It can be noted that numerical equality is the borderline case of proportional equality. For example, if workers in a factory have identical work hours it would be numerical equality. If each worker receives a salary according to their labor, then we are talking about proportional equality. We can be very easily speaking of identity instead of equality. Therefore, good is when the number of work hours is identical for all the workers. Or, good is when the relation between the labor and the salary are identical for each worker.[1] In its pure form, the goodness is a relation of identity.

Let us sum up that with the admitting of equality as an essence of morality, it is admitted that identity is the essence of morality since the essence of equality is identity itself.

5.2 Justice

Justice is one of the most important moral concepts. Its classical definition is "giving every man his due"[2] as we see it in Justinian, and in similar variants, it can also be found in Plato, Aristotle, Aquinas, Augustine, and many others. Justice can be understood as a moral virtue of character and as the desired property of social institutions.[3] I do not believe that there is a fundamental difference between these two natures of justice given that political virtue is based on the moral virtue of character and what is morally bad cannot be politically good. The difference between political macro-relationships and interpersonal micro-relationships is only quantitative. Justice and goodness are very similar concepts and often, especially in the past, they were used as synonyms. In contemporary use good is a broader term than justice and completely encompasses it. Justice usually refers to the distribution of goods and privileges, benefits, and burdens; while violence, lying, or negligence as negative moral phenomena would not be characterized as injustice. In any case, everything just is at the same time good, and this is why it can be said that this metaethical analysis of the nature and origin of justice is at the same time analysis of the goodness. An attempt will be made here to prove that justice is essentially an identity relation.

The most important and fundamental property of justice is equality. Equality is a foundation of justice and irreducible aim of justice. This is the fundamental thesis of the moral egalitarianism, discussed above. The roots of this conception of justice date back to antiquity. In Aristotle's *Nicomachean Ethics* there is an often cited expression that best portrays the foundation of justice:

> Since the unjust man is unequal and the unjust act unequal, it is clear that there is also an intermediate for the unequal. And this is the equal; for in any kind of action in which there is a more and a

---

[1] As early as the Chapter 'Beauty' when I was talking of the golden section it was established that reason is capable of identifying between relations.

[2] LeBar, Mark and Slote, Michael, *Justice as a Virtue*

[3] Ibid

> less, there is also what is equal. If then, the unjust be unequal, the just is equal, as all men suppose it to be, even apart from argument. ...And the same equality will exist between the persons and between the things concerned; for as the latter—the things concerned—are related, so are the former; if they are not equal, they will not have what is equal, but this is the origin of quarrels and complaints—when either equals have and are awarded unequal shares, or unequals equal shares. (*Nicomachean Ethics*, V, 3, 1131a10-25)

As for the opponents of this view, first, there is no essential difference in the conception of justice between egalitarians and anti-egalitarians: "both sides accept justice as proportional equality" (Gosepath, chapter 2.2).

Conversely, as demonstrated above, utilitarians consider utility the foundation of justice, but I deem the connection between these two concepts to be inessential. In analogy with the proclamation of utility as the foundation of justice, it can also be proclaimed as the foundation of beauty because indisputably beauty is beneficial and causes pleasant feelings in us. Or, more specifically, musical rhythm undoubtedly causes us to feel pleasant and is beneficial – is this enough to claim that utility is the foundation of rhythm? Also, the truth is beneficial because, for example, we feel comfortable with someone who speaks the truth versus someone who lies to us, and therefore, in an analogous manner, we can claim that true statements are those that bring us some benefit. It is also certain that there are many things that are beneficial to us, but they have nothing to do with morality. In accordance with the aforementioned I consider utility to be only one of the epithets, properties of justice, which it shares with countless other things and does not tell us anything about its internal nature, i.e. it does not tell us why justice is useful. It is impossible to distinguish justice, in this sense, from other things that benefit us.

It is interesting that Mill even accepts the classical definition of justice according to which „it is considered just to give a person what 'he deserves' and unjust to deny it" (Mill, 1843, 65), as well as its other formulations, from which it can be clearly concluded that justice is essentially equality. However, he rejects the idea of equality as the foundation of justice and declares it "only a particular kind or branch of general utility, and think that its superior binding force requires a totally different origin" (Mill, 62).

In truth, Mill tries to answer this question. He, like David Hume, explains the origin of the usefulness of justice with the feeling of sympathy for others, arguing that the origin of sympathy is not necessary to discuss: "It is natural to resent, and to repel or retaliate, any harm done or attempted against ourselves, or against those with whom we sympathize. The origin of this sentiment it is not necessary here to discuss" (Mill, 1843, 75). He further claims that "this sentiment, in itself, has nothing moral in it" (Mill, 1843, 76). On the contrary, I think that this feeling has to do with morality and that its explanation is necessary. Namely, sympathy is "understanding between people; common feeling."[4] 'Common feeling' means equal feelings and, therefore, sympathy in its essence is a kind of equality, that is, a kind of identity. Thus, unconsciously, Mill again reaches to equality as the foundation of justice.

I completely agree with the thesis of egalitarianism that equality is the basis of justice, but not that equality is irreducible: on the other hand, as it was previously analyzed, the essence of equality is identity, and each equality can easily be reduced to pure identity. Therefore, if so far it was proven that justice is equality, and equality is a relation of identity, then the set goal of proving justice is an identity relation is achieved.

Additionally, let us look at the definitions of the types of justice with the aim to more concretely understand what this identity is comprised of, i.e. what the moral *tertium comparationis* is. Four types of justice are known in theory: distributional, procedural, retributive, and restorative. Distributive justice is about the principles specifying the just distribution of benefits and burdens: "the outcome for which everyone receives their due. A common basis is that persons should be treated equally unless reasons for inequality exist" (Blackburn, 1996). This definition points to the fact that distributive justice is essentially an identity between the values of benefits and burdens the individual receives on the one hand and the value of merits of the individual on the other hand. If, for example, the burden of taxes for a particular business is identical to the values of benefits that the businessman receives from the state then we are talking about distributive justice. Or, if two equal businesses are identically taxed then we are talking about distributive justice. Procedural justice is related to the process used to decide on the distribution of goods. According to its definition, procedural justice is "the element of justice concerned with the application of laws, rather than with the content of the laws themselves. If an unjust law is applied, then procedural justice

---

[4] sympathy is, n." OED Online, Oxford University Press, June 2017, https://en.oxforddictionaries.com/definition/sympathy. Accessed 17 December 2017.

may obtain although the outcome is unjust. Similarly, an irregular procedure might be procedurally unjust, but give the right result on occasion." (Blackburn, 1996). Or, in its essence, procedural justice is a relation of identity between the application of laws during the decision of distribution of goods and resolving disputes for each individual. Furthermore, retributive justice is "the idea of seeking to balance an injustice by rectifying the situation, or by regaining equality that the injustice overturned. It is most simply summed up in the principle of 'an eye for an eye, and a tooth for a tooth'" (Blackburn, 1996). It can be said that retributive justice is essentially a relation of identity between the severity of crime and severity of punishment. And in the end there is restorative justice, although also known as correctional justice: "*principle of corrective justice*, which (in its most influential form) says that an individual has a duty to repair the wrongful losses that his conduct causes" (Coleman at all, chapter 3.1). Similarly, restorative justice is a relation of identity between the extent of damage and the extent of reparation.

There are other concepts of justice whose analysis would take us too far from the main theme, and therefore, we simply will rely on the egalitarian summary – that equality is the general foundation of justice, and from there it is easy to reduce each of them to identity.

Maybe the best generalization of all of these definitions of justice is the classical definition, according to which justice is "the virtue by which all people are given their due." It is best because it encompasses various morally relevant modes of comparison and in this way, justice can be elegantly defined as a relation of identity between the value of the obtained, and the value of the deserved, and if justice is goodness then goodness is a relation of identity. There is a rightful criticism of this definition saying that it is problematic and banal since it is not established according to which criteria is it decided who deserves what, that the definition is not informative, then it does not determine who is competent to 'measure' merit and gain etc. However, these critiques and flaws in the definition are completely irrelevant to this discussion since the sole aim of this work is to prove that justice is a relation of identity while the substance of that identity is not of primary importance. Regardless of the criteria and the manner of appraising merits and gains in various cultures, situations and different moral agents, the principle of identity stands nonetheless.

****

5.3 Golden rule of ethics

Another argument in support of the thesis expressed here can be drawn from a general moral maxim known in the Western culture as the golden rule of ethics according which we can distinguish between right and wrong actions. According to the eminent British philosopher Simon Blackburn, this rule can be "found in some form in almost every ethical tradition, including that of Confucius (551–479 bc)" (Blackburn, 2001, 101). Virtually all big world religions can be included here. "The golden rule is much-reputed for being the most culturally universal ethical tenet in human history" (Puka, para. 3). This universality of the rule suggests that one can search for the essence of the goodness in it.

There are many versions of this fundamental moral rule, and one of the most common is: "Treat others as you want to be treated." It is considered a part of the moral egalitarianism because clearly and undoubtedly calls for equality which, as it was shown above, is identity in its essence. If I were to analyze its formulation I would show that the golden rule is in its essence an identity between the treatment we want to receive, and the treatment others receive from us. Once the reason establishes this identity, it then estimates the treatment as for right. This identity relation is pure goodness.[5]

The golden rule rests on an unexpressed presumption that we are all identical as human beings and that we are all free and rational moral agents. Further, that we share identical values, beliefs, knowledge, tastes, interests, etc. A possible generalization could be that we are all identical in every morally relevant way, that is, what is right/wrong to us is identical with what is right/wrong to the others. And indeed this presumption is mostly true, at least when the general human attributes are concerned. With this in mind, one would presume that a man should know what others like/dislike. It is understandable that the rule does not function when this presumption is incorrect, that is, in situations when the differences between individuals are prominent. John Bernard Shaw ironically notices: "Do not do unto others as you would that they should do unto you. Their tastes may not be the same" (Shaw, 1902, 1). However, this presumed and partially correct empirical identity is not the essence of the rule. The essence is that the rule, that is, the reason requires that 'those that are identical be treated identically'. There is no further analysis of this axiom; it touches the very foundation of reason.

---

[5] Some might argue that empathy is the core of the golden rule but, as we shall see below, empathy is also a relation of identity in its core.

The main thesis of the moral egalitarianism was that equality is the essence of justice; however, as it can be seen from above, equality, that is, identity is also the core of the golden rule. The fact that the framework of this rule surpasses the framework of justice and refers to goodness, in general, is substantial for this work. Namely, above it was noticed that in the usual everyday use of the term 'justice' it refers to the distribution of goods and privileges, while violence, lying, and negligence as negative moral occurrences would not be characterized as injustice. These moral occurrences, however, as well as many others, are encompassed by the golden rule. So, for example, let us be more specific: do not be violent if you don't want others to be violent to you, etc. This fact confirms that equality, that is, identity is not just a foundation of justice, but much more than that – it is the foundation of morality itself. Support for these views is found in Chomsky who claims that: "In fact, one of the, maybe the most, elementary of moral principles is that of universality, that is, If something's right for me, it's right for you; if it's wrong for you, it's wrong for me. Any moral code that is even worth looking at has that at its core somehow" (Chomsky, 2007).

5.4 Categorical imperative

The golden rule of ethics irresistibly reminds of yet another fundamental moral principle, and this is the categorical imperative of Immanuel Kant. It can be defined as a general formula for deciding which actions are morally right. There are three formulations which, as Kant himself claims, have the same meaning. This is his most famous, first formulation: "Act only on that maxim whereby thou canst at the same time will that it should become a universal law" (Kant, 1785, sec. 2).

What would then constitute the difference between these two moral principles? 'Others' in the 'Treat others as you want to be treated' golden rule refers to any 'others', not some specific 'others'. If this rule refers to any 'others' and not some specific 'others', then it surely refers to the entire humanity, and it can become a universal law, accordingly. In this way, one reaches the categorical imperative with which it can be concluded that there is no essential difference between the two moral principles although Kant insists there is one. The note of subjectivity, i.e. personalization of the golden rule is out of the picture since the same can also be addressed to the categorical imperative because if the individual has personalized views of the way in which the others need to treat them, then they can have personalized views of what needs to be a universal law governing entire humanity. For example, a fair amount of people today would like to see women submitting to men as such universal law.

Actually, the request for a universality which exists not only in Kantian but also in many other ethical theories, is a request for identity because the universal, by definition, is but something that all are identical by. It can be concluded that the categorical imperative, which is maybe the most famous philosophical formulation of moral law, is nothing else but a variant of the request for equality, that is, request for identity between all people according to their actions.

5.5 Analysis of ethical categories

„Then again, all the virtues are a beauty of the soul, a beauty authentic beyond any of these others; but how does symmetry enter here? The soul, it is true, is not a simple unity, but still, its virtue cannot have the symmetry of size or of number: what standard of measurement could preside over the compromise or the coalescence of the soul's faculties or purposes?" (Plotinus, First Ennead, Sixth Tractate, Beauty, 1).

The following is an analysis of a few additional moral categories, mainly virtues which are faces of the general goodness, and vices, stripped to their essence so to additionally support the thesis presented here.

- **Truthfulness**: one of the most important virtues is speaking the truth while lying is a type of moral evil. In chapter 3 it was established that the truth is a relation of identity between the 'thought' and 'reality', and lie is a relation of difference. Thence it can be concluded that the moral request for speaking the truth is a request for identity, this time with the emphasis on the practical consequences in human relationships that result from telling lies or telling the truth.

- **Happiness**: it cannot be said that for happiness, as a desired emotional state, there is an exact or a generally accepted definition. It can, however, be said that happiness is achieved with the achieving of our goals, desires, and wishes. According to this, thinking freely, happiness can be defined as a state occurring when the relation of identity between the actual and desired state in a human being is achieved. Sadness and other opposite emotions represent a relation of difference in the same sense.

- **Hypocrisy**: by definition it is "the practice of claiming to have higher standards or more noble beliefs than is the case" (Blackburn, 1996). According to this, hypocrisy, as a negative moral occurrence, can be reduced to a relation of difference between what one individual claims to believe or standards to have and their behavior in that sense.

- **Impartiality:** it is by definition "equal treatment of all rivals or disputants; fairness" (Blackburn, 1996). Equality, which was defined above as the essence of morality, has many faces and as it can be seen from the definition above, impartiality is one of them. It is a form of equality, and with that a form of identity.

- **Discrimination**: "The unjust or prejudicial treatment of different categories of people, especially on the grounds of race, age, or sex" (op. cit.). According to this, discrimination, as a negative moral occurrence is a relation of difference according to treatment or consideration between persons that belong to the one group, class, or category and those that do not. Discrimination is another, this time upturned, face of equality as a moral principle and as opposed to it the good morality calls for equality, that is, identity in treatment.

- **Envy**: "A feeling of discontented or resentful longing aroused by someone else's possessions, qualities, or luck" (op. cit.). According to this, envy appears when the reason of a person establishes a difference between theirs and another's possessions, qualities, or luck while believing they are equal; Or, a difference between what a person has and what they deserve. As a relation of difference envy is a negative emotion.

- **Love**: a plentitude of meanings. In this essay on the human reason it will be discussed of the interpersonal rational love which corresponds to the Greek *philia* and not of to the romantic or sexual attraction which is not an appearance of reason, but often goes hand in hand with the rational love. There is no comprehensive and generally accepted definition of love, but I believe that the essence is best caught in the definition ascribed to Aristotle, according to which, "Love is composed of a single soul inhabiting two bodies." One soul in two bodies means that the bodies are identical according to the souls and according to this love in its essence can be defined as a relation of identity between two souls. The term soul is unclear, however, what is most important for the purpose of this work is that regardless of what our understanding of soul is, love will always remain a relation of identity. The simplest confirmation for this view is the pleasant feeling of deep affection that takes over us when we meet a person with identical interests, views, tastes, desires, etc. This pleasant feeling can be liking, or if it is stronger – love. *Simil simili gaudet*. Striking is the fact that in the English language the root 'like' is used in 'to like someone' and 'looks alike'. Hatred is a relation of difference in the same sense.

In another place, a similar definition is ascribed to Aristotle for friendship too. Diogenes Laertius says: "To the query, "What is a friend?" his reply was, "A single soul dwelling in two bodies." (Diogenes, 468). Aristotle in his *Nicomachean Ethics* distinguished between three types of friendship: based on utility, friendship based on pleasure, and friendship based on goodness. He considers only the third type of friendship to be true, writing that "Perfect friendship is the friendship of men who are good, and alike in excellence" (*Nicomachean Ethics*, VIII, 3., 1156b8). It is easy to establish that 'alike in excellence' is actually an identity according to excellence, that is, that our friendships are based on identities.

- **Solidarity**: it is defined as a "Unity or agreement of feeling or action, especially among individuals with a common interest; mutual support within a group" (Blackburn, 1996). Accordingly, it can be said that in its essence it is a relation of identity in interests among individuals or between members of a group.

- **Empathy**: by definition, it is "the ability to understand and share the feelings of another" (op. cit.). Sharing feelings means having identical feelings and with someone else. According to this, empathy is identification with the other according to the feelings.

- Another important property of men is their nature as social beings, and it is another form of manifestation of the principle of identity and difference. First and foremost, society itself by definition is "The community of people living in a particular country or region and having shared customs, laws, and organizations" (op. cit.). Everything that people share is everything they are identical by.

The formation of social groups is another form of materialization of reason. By definition, a social group is "a number of individuals associated or aggregated together to a greater or lesser degree, either because they share certain features, like class, ethnicity, etc., or (especially Social Sciences) because they are bound together by patterns of interaction." (op. cit.). A social category is "a class or division of people or things regarded as having particular shared characteristics, a collection of people who do not interact but who share similar properties" (op. cit.). It can be easily established from this that the principle of identity and difference is also manifested here with that that each social group, category, or any other form of unity of reason in individuals, is formed on the foundation of some type of identity between individuals that constitute it. For example, family as a social group is formed on the foundation of identity according to ancestry. Ethnical groups are formed on the foundation of identity according to race, language, nationality, or culture, while the social classes are formed on the foundation of identity according to the social and economic status. Political parties are united by the identical interests, identical ideology, etc. Also, society is based on rules and "All rules, by definition, entail a measure of equality. To enforce a rule is to promote equality of behaviour or treatment. ...This applies whether the rules take the form of moral principles and laws, or codes of positive law or the rules of games or conduct adopted by professional associations, religious organisations, political parties, wherever patterns of behaviour can be codified in a more or less systematic manner." (Berlin, 1956, 84-85). If rules promote equality, then, essentially, they promote identity. And if society is based on rules then it is based on the principle of identity.

****

It can be summarized that each moral virtue is identity and each vice is a difference in its essence. Moral virtues are specific terms of the generic goodness, and according to that from here too it can be concluded that the goodness, in general, is a relation of identity in its essence. Human emotions related to the moral behavior, which have their roots in reason, can be defined as names for experiences that arise in revealing the specific identities and differences and are clearly divided into positive and negative, respectively. It is safe to say that there is an undue exaggeration with the insistence on the reason-emotion dualism by many thinkers, for example as it can be noted in Hume and the moral sensitivity in which the emotional genesis of ethical convictions has often been urged as a proof of their irrationality. As opposed to this, I consider emotions to be rational as logical conclusions are. In the end, according to everything stated so far, it can be concluded that human moral reasoning is based on the principle of identity and difference. "The Primal Good and the Primal Beauty have the one dwelling-place" (Plotinus, First Ennead, Sixth Tractate, Beauty, 9), and that dwelling-place is identity.

5.6 On the problem of justification or the source of morality

> Just as one can ask, "Why be concerned with equality per se?" and "Why weight the interests of the worse-off more heavily?" so one can ask, "Why care about equality of moral status or 'complex' inequalities?" Answers to ethical questions give out when one reaches fundamental notions, and we think that at this point one is close to the foundations of morality (Hausman; McPherson, 2006, 195).

The problem of justification and the source of morality is a complex issue whose thorough analysis would require much more space and time, however, in this regard, an idea imposes an irresistible need to share. As a logical sequel to the nature of morality described above, an answer will be offered to the metaethical problems which refer to the source and the foundation of morality, as well as to the question of the of moral judgment justification. I consider all these metaethical problems to be closely related and their solutions stem from one another from a common source which I will allow myself to call *identity drive*. The essence of equality is identity, and the identity drive represents a foundation of morality; It is at the same time the source of morality explaining and providing justification to any moral judgment. If the actions lead to an identity in a morally relevant sense, then they are morally good and vice versa, if they lead to difference, then they are morally wrong. The strongest illustration of the striving toward identity can be found in the following simple example: if a single cake is to be divided among ten people, then it is completely natural, and there is nothing more natural than cutting the cake in ten identical pieces. Asking the question why is the division in identical parts so natural seems so banal and trivial because it means touching the very essence of our reason and with that to what is self-explanatory. The answer is because the reason is of such nature that strives toward and exists through the identities and this is the special cause for the need to divide the cake into identical pieces. This striving for identities is what Plato calls 'health of the soul'.[6] I am convinced that we are speaking the same thing.

The human spirit lives through identities, and they are its being as opposed to the differences because of which it decays; experiencing identities and differences is accompanied by emotional responses, positive or negative, respectively. The reason is connected to the body through the brain, and the experiencing of identities and differences through which the spirit grows and parishes are reflected in the body in the form of emotions.

Moral behavior is completely founded on the drive for identities. This drive provides us with the motivation for moral action, and its satisfaction is a reward in itself. A person does not have to try hard to be moral or to be moral because they expect some kind of a reward for their actions. Pleasant emotions we have when the reason experiences identities and respect from the others toward the person whose actions lead to identities is a reward in itself. Striving for identity is a goal of its own, not an instrument worthy because of the consequences it produces. It is the

---

[6] Namely, analyzing why justice would have an advantage over injustice Plato writes: ""'isn't to produce justice to establish the parts of the soul in a relation of mastering, and being mastered by, one another that is according to nature, while to produce injustice is to establish a relation of ruling, and being ruled by, one another that is contrary to nature?" ..."Virtue, then, as it seems, would be certain health, beauty and good condition of the soul, and vice a sickness, ugliness and weakness."" (*The Republic of Plato*, book IV, 124)

final goal of the rational moral action. These views coincide with the view of the so-called intrinsic egalitarians according to which 'equality is an intrinsic good in itself', even if it means 'levelling-down'. Let us, for example, consider cases when the immediate family of a child that lost its hair due to illness also shave their heads, and by this, they achieve a relation of identity with their child. This relation of identity is a clear example of moral good. Another extreme example in the same sense is when the moral agent achieves a relation of identity by taking their own life after the death of the one they loved.

The subject here is rational morality, i.e. what is good according to reason; man, however, as a whole, is much more than just reason. Namely, aside from the drive for identities, there are biological drives and bodily needs such as survival, hunger, the absence of pain, sexual needs, which are often in conflict with the rational needs. The identity drive is of course in a constant struggle with the remaining natural drives which together shape our complex nature. The term 'good' in its everyday use is alternately used both in reasonable and in the biological sense. Therefore I consider that there is a need of distinguishing between reasonable good/bad and biological good/bad. The first denotes satisfying/not satisfying the needs of the reason, while the other denotes satisfying/not satisfying biological needs. This distinction can be elaborated with one example: if ten thirsty people share a liter of water in ten equal parts, their reasonable needs will be satisfied for there is an identity between the quantity of water that each one of them got, and this act is valued as good. Their biological needs, however, remain unsatisfied and this is valued as bad. If one does not get their tenth, then their biological and their rational needs have not been satisfied. If, on the other hand, ten thirsty people share twenty liters of water, and each one of them receives two liters, then both the rational and the biological needs of everyone will be satisfied. If one of them receives only one liter of water and the others get two, then their rational needs will not be satisfied regardless of them having enough to satisfy their biological need for water.

There are also moral principles that result and are based on biological drives, not less important than the rational, as for example outlawing murder, the affliction of physical harm, etc. In some way, the drive for identity, i.e. pure rational goodness, intertwines with the biological good. It seems that the biological drives, as well as other attributes, composting human nature, result in the modes according to which the reason establishes identities between the moral agents – they provide substance to the pure reasonable morality.

Morality always refers to actions, and the good or the bad are epithets for the actions, i.e. the individual or institutions that perform them. Considering the fact that the good is not a property, such as it is, for example, color of material objects, but it is a relation established by reason, it can be said that not one action can be good or bad in itself. The action is good only if its consequence is a type of identity between states of affairs of the human individuals in certain situations. Similarly, as not one element of the structure of the aesthetical object is beautiful in itself, but only in its relation to other elements of the object.

The moral good does not vary from person to person, or from culture to culture, so I cannot call myself moral relativist or subjectivist because the principle on which the reason functions and the identity drive are common to every person in every culture. Where do then differences in moral judgments among various people, which obviously exist, come from? Individual or collective moral agents can be differentiated according to the valuation, that is, estimation of things that need to be equated, such as for example are merits and gain. Further, they can be differentiated according to priorities of identification as for example in complex situations when there is the need to choose between two goods, i.e. between two identities in which they want the action to result. It is certain that not all identities have the same values. In different situations and according to various moral agents a different kind of identity prevails as the most important, and accordingly, it imposes as a priority principle of the decision-making process as opposed to other possible identities that remain secondary and are overlooked. The differences can also appear according to the question of between who is the identity supposed to be established and when. I will not go further into substantial moral inquires here. This inquiry is essentially reduced to a search of rightful valuation, estimation, and setting priorities for things that enter into the identity relation in a moral sense. Regardless of these differences the principle of identity according to which the good is being established remains the common point always in all rational moral agents. Immorality, on the other hand, results from ignorance, the weak reason that cannot estimate and evaluate or is unfamiliar with the modes according to which it needs to identify, and it cannot foresee the consequences from the actions it takes, accordingly. Another source of immorality would be suppression of the rationale for the sake of satisfying the biological drives or some other goals. Evil is irrational.

Let us summarize that the sources and the foundation of morality is the *drive for identity* and according to this each moral virtue, up to and including goodness itself, is a name for a certain type of identity relation.

Moral reasoning, which is in search of these identities, reduces to identification and differentiation in its essence. Identity is an absolute and universal principle, and the complete history of morality, all moral laws, rules, norms, are but attempts for it to be rightfully specified in various areas, sometimes successfully, other times not as much. This is one attempt to bridge over the worries of metaethicians that there is no way of justifying assumptions and commitments stemming from morality. Morality is not a myth, but a materialization of reason in the sphere of human relationships.

Philosophical Monolith

Dear reader, we need to establish the general conclusion which, I believe, you yourself already arrived at. Let us repeat the main conclusions derived here from the examination of the human reason in its most general areas of appearance following the order of the chapters. Their true meaning cannot be entirely comprehended in their individuality but in their unity which gives them mutual confirmation:

1. Reason cognizes things on the principle of identity and difference;
2. Reason thinks on the principle of identity and difference;
3. Reason cognizes truth on the principle of identity and difference;
4. Reason cognizes and creates beauty on the principle of identity and difference;
5. Reason acts morally on the principle of identity and difference.

These five forms of appearance of the reason in their generality encompass almost the complete activity of the reason and their analysis, accordingly, is enough for making a general conclusion: reason functions on the principle of identity and difference. At its deepest level, the reason is the identification-differentiation ability; and all appearances of reason are manifestations of this same essence. This is how everything is connected.

Of course that this conclusion itself is an act of reason, as is the entire theory presented here, and according to this, if I am to be consistent, they too need to be manifestations of the principle of identity and difference. And it is so – on a metalevel this general conclusion is actually identification between individual conclusions, and the essence of this theory is the understanding of the relation of identity between the plenitude of appearances of reason: all appearances of reason are the same according to the fact that they are all different manifestations of the principle of identity and difference. This reasoning is an element of self-awareness, reason of reason itself.

Based on everything said until now an ontological classification of things as we know them, i.e. reality as we know it, is offered. Aside from cognizing the objective reality which was the topic of discussion in the first chapter reason possesses another fascinating ability to cognize itself. Namely, the reason is able to cognize and name as things the operations that itself performs and relations that it establishes, an ability which I call metacognition. According to this, I suggest two sources for our entire knowledge: the first type of knowledge we obtain through the reflection of reason on objective reality, i.e. through processing of material provided by the senses; and the second through the auto-reflection of reason on itself. The external world is the object of cognition in the first source, while in the second the reason adopts itself as an object of cognition. In accordance with this differentiation, one can argue that there are two types of universal things in reality as we know it which I will call ideas and meta-ideas. Things – ideas are a product of the process of cognition of the external reality, and meta-ideas are a product of the process of cognition of reason itself. Things – ideas are either particular spatial-temporal sequences obtained with the processing of identity-difference of the material provided by our senses or are universal and obtained through identity-difference processing of particular things as it was described in the first chapter. Cognition of ideas actually is *a posteriori* cognition. On the other hand, meta-ideas which were the topic of discussion in the rest of the work can be divided into operations and relations. Meta-ideas-operations are names for identifications and differentiations themselves performed by the reason, while meta-ideas-relations are names of identities and differences themselves that the reason establishes between things. Meta-ideas can be both universals, and particular things wherein universals have names while individual operations or relations we do not have the practice of naming, as it is sometimes the case with particular things – ideas. For their cognition, we do not need sensory experience, and therefore it can be said that the cognition of meta-ideas is *a priori* cognition, i.e. these are things that do not correspond to anything in reality in itself. Meta-ideas are cognition of the reason to itself, cognition of cognition itself, i.e. they are, I would say, elements of self-awareness. The reason that knows of meta-ideas is a reason that knows itself.

If the reason is an ability of identification and differentiation, then our spirit is a sum of identities that the reason establishes. Reason lives only when it identifies and differentiates, and the greatness of the spirit is as big as the identities that the reason has established. The tissue of the human spirit is composed of its identities, and it grows with them as opposed to the differences through which it fades. The spirit enjoys the identities, it exists through them and therefore it can be said that there is a fundamental human drive for identities.[1] The identity drive is not only the source and foundation of moral actions, as it was previously established, but it is a universal propellant of reason. Goodness, beauty, and truth together compose the trinity of highest philosophical values of which it can be said that are generic terms of their own, encompassing all other human values. As it was seen, these are just different types of identity relations with which it becomes clear why they are often considered synonyms in the history of philosophy. Truth is beauty and beauty is goodness, and when we wish for and strive for goodness, beauty, truth, knowledge, happiness when we love, then we strive for a certain identity. Experiencing identities is accompanied by positive emotions, regardless of whether they are in the form of beauty,[2] good, or truth. In this way, the striving for identities can be set as the propellant of life, as will. Striving for identities is a goal in itself that does not have justification in anything higher than itself, it is a rational drive of its own kind different than other drives that compose our libido, sometimes in accordance with them, sometimes opposing them.

If one identity is an elementary and indivisible unit, i.e. an atom of the human spirit, then one comparison is the basic, elementary, and indivisible unit, i.e. the atom of reason. Behind the unimaginable complexity of reason functioning stands a simple atomary identification and differentiation that in its countless combinations and variations produces this complexity. It seems certain that this elementary cell of the reason has its material foundation, i.e. that a type of material process in the brain corresponds to identification and differentiation, the discovery of which remains the task of neurophysiologists.

Things exist only as opposed to the different from themselves. Differences create things and things create differences. Let us imagine a red

---

[1] Similar thoughts can be found in Nietzsche: "On the understanding of *logic:* : : *the will to sameness is the will to power.*" (Nietzsche, 1886, Notebook 2, para. 90, 77). The act of presenting this thought here is itself a manifestation of this *drive for identities*. The pleasure it gives is its satisfaction.

[2] Or, in Plotinus's words, when the soul recognizes beauty „welcomes it, enters into unison with it. But let the soul fall in with the Ugly and at once it shrinks within itself, denies the thing, turns away from it, not accordant, resenting it. Our interpretation is that the soul- by the very truth of its nature, by its affiliation to the noblest Existents in the hierarchy of Being- when it sees anything of that kin, or any trace of that kinship, thrills with an immediate delight, takes its own to itself, and thus stirs anew to the sense of its nature and of all its affinity " (First Ennead, Sixth Tractate, Beauty, 2)

dot on a yellow surface. The red dot exists only because of the yellow background from which it is different. If we replace the different background with non-different (non-different from yellow is yellow), then the dot will seize to exist as an entity. And the background itself will seize to exist because the background exists only as different to the 'foreground'. It is meaningless to say for a purely yellow piece of paper that it is a yellow background because it does not have something to be the background too. This view takes us to dialectical laws. In the same sense war exists only as opposed to peace, light exists only opposed to dark, and the truth only as opposed to the lie. In this case, the red and the yellow are not opposite, but simply different. Thence can be said that the law on the unity and the battle of the opposites can be enhanced to become law on the unity and the battle of the differences. It seems that opposites are only specific types of elementary differences. Their battle consists of the fact that the existence of the one thing negates the existence of the other thing, i.e. with the increase of the quantity of the one thing, the quantity of the other thing decreases and vice versa. However, although through battle, they exist only together. If the quantity of the one thing reaches a certain upper limit to negate and destroy the other thing completely, it will destroy itself by doing so, and other qualities will ensue. What would be the sense of the truth as a concept if there is no lie, or what would peace be without war? On a meta level, dialectical laws themselves are nothing but a relation of identity according to relations that exist between all different types of opposites.

From this set of things, one can argue that primordial knowledge is knowledge of two things simultaneously and that each act of cognition is cognition of a minimum of two things simultaneously. It is so because cognition functions on the principle of identity and difference, and this principle implies identification and differentiation which is impossible without a minimum of two things. This means that everything that we know exists only as opposed to something different than it. Identification in itself and differentiation from otherness on which cognition is founded are opposite and simultaneous operations, two names of the same operation, same operation from a different point of view, as the way up and the way down are one and the same. Ultimate uniformity or difference of reality means death to reason.

If this theory presented here proves to be true, social consequences would be immeasurable. The idea for the creation of an artificial reason can become a reality. If for example a machine is designed to be capable of identification and differentiation in the structure of an electrical impulse, as well as connecting identities in themselves in larger groups, then this machine would be capable of generating particular and universal things, or in other words – to cognize. I am convinced that the most striking and relatively easiest confirmation of this theory can be achieved through analysis of music, i.e. melody since it is the most abstract of arts – pure form. The melody is a structure consisting of a series of consequential tones and rests. What is interesting for melody is the fact that the tones can be identified and differentiated according to only two modes – duration and height for the tones, and the rests can be identified or differentiated only according to their duration. The timbre of the sound as a mode of differentiation is excluded since melody retains its beauty if it is played in a different instrument. This fact greatly simplifies things and enables us to most easily establish and count the relations of identity existing in such structure in comparison to other arts. What we need to do is choose melodies for which there is general consent regarding their beauty and to establish their identity-difference structure. This means to establish the duration and height of each tone and each rest individually and then count and position all relations of identity and difference existing in these structures. I propose that the best way to do this is to graphically, i.e. visually present melody. Notions acquired with this analysis will allow us to create similar or analogous identity-difference structures artificially. These artificial structures should, if this theory is correct, to be similarly or identically beautiful which would actually mean that beauty was artificially created. "Music is a hidden arithmetic exercise of the soul, which does not know that it is counting" (Leibniz, 1712, 241). If the test is successful, this would mean a possibility for the artificial creation of music the beauty of which would be with so great and a maybe unknown intensity, and with that death to music as we know it. If we succeed in causing music to die in this way, it will be a clear sign that we have discovered the secret of the functioning of reason.

Mark Twain's doctor kept him on a strict diet that consisted only of one glass of milk and a few pieces of bread and toast each day. "Since I've got nothing else to eat, give me a couple of postage stamps: I want to do some reading before going to bed." The spirit of this anecdote, the essence of its beauty and the pleasure it produces is meta identity: the relation between the allowed quantity of food and the actual needs of Twain is identical to the relation between the quantity of text he suggests and his usual needs for reading. The essence of the anecdote is rationalized at the cost of destroying it.

Bibliography

1. Aristotle, *Metaphysics*, in *The complete works of Aristotle*, The Revised Oxford Translation, vol. 2, ed. Jonathan Barnes, Electronic Edition, Princeton: Princeton University Press, 1984.
2. — —, *Nicomachean Ethics*, in *The complete works of Aristotle*, The Revised Oxford Translation, vol. 2, ed. Jonathan Barnes, Electronic Edition, Princeton: Princeton University Press, 1984.
3. — —, *On Memory*, in *The complete works of Aristotle*, The Revised Oxford Translation, vol. 1, ed. Jonathan Barnes, Electronic Edition, Princeton: Princeton University Press, 1984.
4. — —, *Politics*, in *The Complete Works of Aristotle*, The Revised Oxford Translation, vol. 2, ed. Jonathan Barnes, Electronic Edition, Princeton: Princeton University Press, 1984.
5. Arneson, Richard, "Egalitarianism", *The Stanford Encyclopedia of Philosophy* (Summer 2013 Edition), Edward N. Zalta (ed.), URL = <https://plato.stanford.edu/archives/sum2013/entries/egalitarianism/>.
6. Ashworth, E. Jennifer, "Medieval Theories of Analogy", *The Stanford Encyclopedia of Philosophy (Fall 2015 Edition)*, Edward N. Zalta (ed.), URL = <http://plato.stanford.edu/archives/fall2015/entries/analogy-medieval/>.
7. Baldick, Chris, 2001, *The Concise Oxford Dictionary of Literary Terms*, New York: Oxford University Press.
8. Bartha, Paul, "Analogy and Analogical Reasoning", *The Stanford Encyclopedia of Philosophy (Fall 2015 Edition)*, Edward N. Zalta (ed.), URL = <http://plato.stanford.edu/archives/fall2015/entries/reasoning-analogy/>.
9. Baudelaire, Charles, [1863], *The Painter of Modern Life, and other essays*, trans. Jonathan Mayne, London: Phaidon Press [1964], Retrieved February 11, 2016 from <http://www.columbia.edu/itc/architecture/ockman/pdfs/dossier_4/Baudelaire.pdf>.
10. Beaney, Michael, "Analysis", *The Stanford Encyclopedia of Philosophy (Fall 2015 Edition)*, Edward N. Zalta (ed.), URL = <http://plato.stanford.edu/archives/fall2015/entries/analysis/>.
11. Berlin, Isaiah, [1956], "Equality" in *Concepts and Categories: Philosophical Essays*, ed. Henry Hardy, London: Pimlico, 1999, pp. 81 – 102.

12. Blackburn, Simon, 1996, *Oxford Dictionary of Philosophy (Oxford Paperback Reference)*, Oxford: Oxford University Press.
13. Blackburn, Simon, 2001, *Ethics: A Very Short Introduction*, Oxford: Oxford University Press, Retrieved January 11, 2016, from <http://www.zbmu.ac.ir/files/Medical%20Ethics/pages/ethics_vsi.pdf>.
14. BonJour, Laurence, "Epistemological Problems of Perception", *The Stanford Encyclopedia of Philosophy (Fall 2015 Edition)*, Edward N. Zalta (ed.), URL = <http://plato.stanford.edu/archives/fall2015/entries/perception-episprob/>.
15. Cabrera Research Lab, "Every Metaphor and Simile has an Analogy Inside", Online video clip, YouTube, August 6, 2008. Retrieved December 12, 2015, from <https://www.youtube.com/watch?v=VhueKrKKNps>.
16. Candlish, Stewart; Damnjanovic, Nic, "The Identity Theory of Truth", *The Stanford Encyclopedia of Philosophy (Winter 2012 Edition)*, Edward N. Zalta (ed.), URL = <http://plato.stanford.edu/archives/win2012/entries/truth-identity/>.
17. Chalmers, David J., Robert M. French and Douglas R. Hofstadter, 1991, "High-Level Perception, Representation, and Analogy: A Critique of Artificial Intelligence Methodology", *Journal of Experimental and Theoretical Artificial Intelligence*, [Vol. 4, Iss. 3, 1992], Center for Research on Concepts and Cognition Indiana University, Retrieved December 12, 2015, from <http://consc.net/papers/highlevel.pdf>.
18. Chomsky, Noam, 2007, August 3, "On Responsibility, War Guilt and Intellectuals", *CounterPunch*, Retrieved January 12, 2016, from <http://www.counterpunch.org/2007/08/03/on-responsibility-war-guilt-and-intellectuals/>.
19. Cohen, Morris R. and Ernest Nagel, [1934], *An Introduction to Logic and Scientific Method*, Allied publishers: New Delhi, 1968.
20. Coleman, Jules, Hershovitz, Scott and Mendlow, Gabriel, "Theories of the Common Law of Torts", *The Stanford Encyclopedia of Philosophy* (Winter 2015 Edition), Edward N. Zalta (ed.), URL = <https://plato.stanford.edu/archives/win2015/entries/tort-theories/>.
21. Coleridge, Samuel Taylor, [1836], *The Literary Remains of Samuel Taylor Coleridge*, vol. 1, ed. Henry Nelson Coleridge and Esq. M. A, Produced by Jonathan Ingram, et al., Project Gutenberg, Retrieved January 07, 2016, from <http://www.gutenberg.org/files/8488/8488-h/8488-h.htm#section47>.
22. Cook, Roy T., 2009, *A Dictionary of Philosophical Logic*, Edinburgh: Edinburgh University Press.

23. Crane, Tim, "The Problem of Perception", *The Stanford Encyclopedia of Philosophy (Fall 2015 Edition)*, Edward N. Zalta (ed.), URL = <http://plato.stanford.edu/archives/fall2015/entries/perception-problem/>.
24. David, Marian, "The Correspondence Theory of Truth", *The Stanford Encyclopedia of Philosophy* (Fall 2015 Edition), Edward N. Zalta (ed.), URL = <http://plato.stanford.edu/archives/fall2015/entries/truth-correspondence/>.
25. Diogenes Laertius, *Lives of Eminent Philosophers*, trans. R.D. Hicks, vol. 1, Cambridge: Harvard University Press, 1959.
26. Dworkin, Ronald, 2000, *Sovereign Virtue. The Theory and Practice of Equality*, Cambridge: Harvard University Press.
27. Euclid, *The Thirteen Books of the Elements*, trans. Thomas L. Heath, vol. 1, 2nd ed., Cambridge: Cambridge University Press, 1908.
28. Forrest, Peter, "The Identity of Indiscernibles", *The Stanford Encyclopedia of Philosophy* (Winter 2016 Edition), Edward N. Zalta (ed.), URL = <https://plato.stanford.edu/archives/win2016/entries/identity-indiscernible/>.
29. Frege, Gottlob, 1918, "Thought", trans. Peter Geach and R. H. Stoothoff in Michael Beany, ed. *The Frege Reader*, Oxford: Blackwell, 1997, pp. 325-345.
30. Geach, P.T., 1972. *Logic Matters*, Oxford: Basil Blackwell.
31. Gentner, Dedre, Keith J. Holyoak and Boicho N. Kokinov, eds., 2001, *The Analogical Mind: Perspectives from Cognitive Science*, Cambridge MA: The MIT Press/Bradford Book.
32. Glanzberg, Michael, "Truth", *The Stanford Encyclopedia of Philosophy (Fall 2015 Edition)*, Edward N. Zalta (ed.), URL = <http://plato.stanford.edu/archives/fall2015/entries/truth/>.
33. Gosepath, Stefan, "Equality", *The Stanford Encyclopedia of Philosophy (Winter 2015 Edition)*, Edward N. Zalta (ed.), URL = <http://plato.stanford.edu/archives/win2015/entries/equality/>.
34. Gosepath, Stefan, "Equality", *The Stanford Encyclopedia of Philosophy* (Spring 2011 Edition), Edward N. Zalta (ed.), URL = <https://plato.stanford.edu/archives/spr2011/entries/equality/>.
35. Griffin, James, 1986, *Well-Being: Its Meaning, Measurement and Moral Importance*, Oxford: Clarendon Press.
36. Hausman, Daniel M. and Michael S. McPherson, 2006, *Economic Analysis, Moral Philosophy, and Public Policy*, 2nd ed, Cambridge: Cambridge University Press.
37. Heidegger, Martin, [1962], *What is a Thing*, trans. W.B. Barton, Jr. and V. Deutsch, South Bend, Indiana: Gateway Editions, 1967, (First published in German as *Die Frage nach dem Ding*).
38. Heidegger, Martin, 1957, *Identity and Difference*, trans. Joan Stambaugh, 1 ed., New York: Harper & Row, 1969.

39. Heisenberg, Werner, 1958, *Physics and Philosophy: The Revolution in Modern Science*, London: George Allen & Unwin, 1971, Retrieved January 17, 2016, from <https://archive.org/details/PhysicsPhilosophy>.
40. Hume, David, 1739 - 40, *A Treatise of Human Nature*, vol. 1, ed. David Fate Norton and Mary J. Norton, Oxford: Clarendon Press, 2007.
41. Hume, David, 1748, *An Enquiry Concerning Human Understanding*, ed. Peter Millican, Oxford: Oxford University Press, 2007.
42. Husserl, Edmund, [1907], *The Idea of Phenomenology*, in *Husserliana: Edmund Husserl - Collected Works*, vol. VIII, trans. Lee Hardy, Dordrecht: Kluwer Academic Publishers 1999.
43. Hutcheson, Francis, 1726, *An Inquiry into the Original of Our Ideas of Beauty and Virtue in Two Treatises*, ed. Wolfgang Leidhold, Indianapolis: Liberty Fund, 2004, Retrieved January 05, 2016, from <http://oll.libertyfund.org/titles/2462#lf1458_label_073>.
44. Kandel, Eric R., Schwartz, James H., Jessell and Thomas M. eds., 2000, *Principles of Neural Science*, 4th_Ed, U.S.A.: McGraw-Hill Medical.
45. Kant, Immanuel, [1785], *Fundamental Principles of the Metaphysic of Morals*, trans. Thomas Kingsmill Abbott, eBooks @ Adelaide, 2014, Retrieved January 13, 2016, from <https://ebooks.adelaide.edu.au/k/kant/immanuel/k16prm/chapter2.html>.
46. Kant, Immanuel, 1783, *Prolegomena to Any Future Metaphysics*, trans. and ed. Gary Hatfield, Revised Edition, Cambridge: Cambridge University Press, 2004.
47. Kant, Immanuel, 1787, *The Critique of Pure Reason*, in *The Cambridge Edition of the Works of Immanuel Kant*, trans. and ed. Paul Guyer and Allen W. Wood, Cambridge: Cambridge University Press, 1998.
48. Kant, Immanuel, 1790, *Critique of Judgement*, trans. James Creed Meredith, ed. Nicholas Walker, Oxford: Oxford University Press, 2007.
49. LeBar, Mark and Slote, Michael, "Justice as a Virtue", *The Stanford Encyclopedia of Philosophy* (Spring 2016 Edition), Edward N. Zalta (ed.), URL = <https://plato.stanford.edu/archives/spr2016/entries/justice-virtue/>.
50. Leibniz, Gottfried Wilhelm, "Letter to Christian Goldbach" [1712], in *Epistolae ad diversos*, Lipsiae, [1734], pp. 239-242, Retrieved June 30, 2016, from: <http://reader.digitale-sammlungen.de/de/fs1/object/display/bsb10403201_00279.html>.
51. Livio, Mario, 2002, *The Golden Ratio: The Story of Phi, the World's Most Astonishing Number*, New York: Broadway Books.

52. Locke, John, [1689], *An Essay Concerning Human Understanding*, eBooks @ Adelaide, 2015, Retrieved December 27, 2015, from <https://ebooks.adelaide.edu.au/l/locke/john/l81u/index.html>.
53. Markie, Peter, "Rationalism vs. Empiricism", *The Stanford Encyclopedia of Philosophy (Fall 2015 Edition)*, Edward N. Zalta (ed.), URL = <http://plato.stanford.edu/archives/fall2015/entries/rationalism-empiricism/>.
54. Mill, John Stuart, 1843, *A System of Logic Ratiocinative and Inductive, Being a connected view of the Principles of Evidence, and the Methods of Scientific Investigation*, in *The Collected works of John Stuart Mill*, ed. J. M. Robson, vol. VII, Toronto: University of Toronto Press, London: Routledge & Kegan Paul, 1974.
55. Mill, John Stuart, 1863, *Utilitarianism*, London: Parker, Son, and Bourn.
56. Miller, David, 1997, "Equality and Justice," in: *Ratio: An International Journal of Analytic Philosophy*, Vol. 10, No. 3, 222-237.
57. Nietzsche, Friedrich, 1886, *Writings from the Late Notebooks*, ed. Rüdiger Bittner, trans. Kate Sturge, Cambridge: Cambridge University Press, 2003.
58. Nietzsche, Friedrich, 1901, *The Will to Power*, ed. Walter Kaufmann, trans. Walter Kaufmann and R. J. Hollingdale, 1st ed., New York: Vintage Books, 1968.
59. Noonan, Harold and Curtis, Ben, "Identity", *The Stanford Encyclopedia of Philosophy* (Spring 2017 Edition), Edward N. Zalta (ed.), URL = <https://plato.stanford.edu/archives/spr2017/entries/identity/>.
60. Plato, *The Republic of Plato*, trans. Allan Bloom, 2nd ed., The United States: Basic Books, 1991.
61. Plotinus, *The Six Enneads*, trans. by Stephen MacKenna and B. S. Page, eBooks @ Adelaide, 2014, Retrieved December 06, 2015, from <https://ebooks.adelaide.edu.au/p/plotinus/p72e/>.
62. Puka, Bill, "The Golden Rule", *The Internet Encyclopedia of Philosophy*, ISSN 2161-0002. Retrieved January 11, 2016, from <http://www.iep.utm.edu/goldrule/#H4>.
63. Quincey, Christian de, 2010, *Radical Nature: The Soul of Matter*, 2nd ed. Rochester, Vermont: Park Street Press.
64. Quine, Willard Van Orman, 1963, *From a logical point of view: 9 logico-philosophical essays*, 2nd ed. revised, New York: Harper & Row Publishers.
65. Rand, Ayn, 1964, *The Virtue of Selfishness: A New Concept of Egoism*, New York: Signet Books, Retrieved July 25, 2016, from <http://www.e-reading.club/bookreader.php/137212/Rand_-_The_Virtue_of_Selfishness.pdf>.
66. Russell, Bertrand, [1912], *The Problems of Philosophy*, Produced by Gordon Keener, and David Widger, Project Gutenberg, Re-

trieved July 5, 2016, from
<http://www.gutenberg.org/files/5827/5827-h/5827-h.htm>.
67. Russell, Bertrand, 1940, *An Inquiry into Meaning and Truth*, London: Allen and Unwin.
68. Sartwell, Crispin, "Beauty", *The Stanford Encyclopedia of Philosophy (Fall 2015 Edition)*, Edward N. Zalta (ed.), URL = <http://plato.stanford.edu/archives/fall2015/entries/beauty/>.
69. Shaw, George Bernard, [1902], *Maxims for Revolutionists*, Produced by Russell Bell, Project Gutenberg, Retrieved January 11, 2016, from <http://archive.org/stream/maximsforrevolut26107gut/26107.txt>
70. Shelley, Cameron, 2003, *Multiple analogies in Science and Philosophy*, Amsterdam: John Benjamins Publishing Company.
71. Spinoza, Benedict de. [1677], *A Spinoza Reader: The Ethics and Other Works*, trans. and ed. Edwin Curley, Princeton: Princeton University Press, 1994.
72. Todorovic, Dejan, 2008, "Gestalt principles", Scholarpedia, 3(12):5345, Retrieved December 06, 2015, from <http://www.scholarpedia.org/article/Gestalt_principles>.
73. Vitruvius, [1486], *Ten Books on Architecture*, trans. Morris N. Morgan, Cambridge: Harvard University Press, 1914, Project Gutenberg, Produced by Chuck Greif et al., Retrieved January 02, 2016, from <http://www.gutenberg.org/files/20239/20239-h/29239-h.htm>.
74. Warren, Howard C., 1921, *A History of the Association Psychology*, New York: Charles Scribner's sons.
75. Wölfflin, Heinrich, 1932, *Principles of Art History: The Problem of the Development of Style in Later Art*, trans. M. D. Hottinger, New York: Dover, 1950, The Internet Archive, Retrieved January 03, 2016, from <https://archive.org/details/princarth00wlff>.
76. Јосифовски, Јонче, 1984, *Историја на логиката*, Скопје: Универзитет Кирил и Методиј.

Index

A

analogy, 40, 41, 42, 43, 44, 82, 98
analysis, viii, 6, 8, 10, 17, 23, 27, 28, 34, 36, 37, 39, 41, 44, 45, 46, 47, 48, 49, 61, 62, 73, 75, 83, 84, 91, 97, 100, 101, 103, 106, 111, 115
anaphora, 78
Aristotle, 41, 43, 48, 49, 60, 74, 104
association, 48, 49, 50, 51, 52, 53, 79
assonance, 79
Ayn Rand, vii

B

Bartha, Paul, 41, 42
Baudelaire, Charles, 85
beauty, vii, viii, 73, 74, 75, 76, 77, 80, 81, 82, 83, 84, 85, 86, 87, 88, 89, 90, 98, 103, 107, 111, 113, 115
being, 5, vii, 1, 3, 4, 9, 13, 14, 18, 19, 20, 22, 27, 30, 31, 33, 35, 37, 39, 40, 45, 63, 67, 69, 74, 75, 78, 79, 80, 84, 87, 88, 89, 93, 95, 101, 103, 107, 109
Berkeley, George, 48, 68
Berlin, Isaiah, 106
Blackburn, Simon, 3, 53, 99, 101, 103, 105
BonJour, Laurence, 6, 7, 8, 65, 66, 67

C

Chalmers, David, 43
Chomsky, Noam, 102
cognition, 1, 2, 4, 5, 6, 8, 14, 15, 18, 21, 23, 24, 25, 26, 27, 28, 31, 32, 33, 34, 35, 40, 42, 44, 59, 67, 69, 70, 86, 88, 112, 114
Coleridge, Samuel Taylor, 83
correspondence, 59, 60, 61, 62, 70, 80
Crane, Tim, 7, 67, 68

D

deduction, 37, 39, 45
Descartes, René, 2
dialectical, 20, 22, 46, 56, 114
difference, ix, 11, 12, 18, 19, 20, 21, 22, 23, 24, 26, 27, 29, 31, 33, 34, 37, 38, 39, 40, 45, 48, 52, 54, 55, 56, 57, 60, 62, 63, 64, 65, 66, 67, 68, 69, 70, 76, 78, 82, 83, 84, 85, 88, 97, 98, 102, 103, 104, 105, 106, 107, 111, 112, 114, 115

E

electrical impulses, 2, 4, 6, 7, 8, 14, 15, 18, 23, 25, 27, 31, 85
empathy, 101, 105
epistemology, ix, 1, 7, 67
epistrophe, 78
equality, 91, 92, 93, 94, 95, 96, 97, 98, 99, 100, 101, 102, 103, 104, 105, 106, 107, 108

Eric, Kandel, 29
Euclid, 39, 45, 46, 47, 76

G

Gestalt theory, 27, 29
golden section, 76, 79, 97
goodness, 82, 91, 95, 96, 97, 100, 101, 103, 105, 106, 108, 109, 113

H

harmony, vii, 74, 80, 81, 82, 90
Hausman, 106
Heidegger, Martin, 9, 14
Heisenberg, Werner, 8
Hofstadter, Douglas, 40, 43
Hume, David, 7, 35, 36, 41, 48, 49, 50, 52, 53, 63, 64, 66, 68, 106
Husserl, Edmund, 26
Hutcheson, Francis, 82

I

identity, ix, 9, 10, 11, 12, 13, 14, 15, 18, 20, 21, 22, 23, 24, 26, 27, 29, 30, 31, 32, 33, 34, 36, 37, 38, 39, 41, 42, 43, 44, 45, 46, 47, 48, 50, 51, 52, 53, 54, 55, 56, 59, 60, 61, 62, 63, 64, 70, 71, 73, 75, 76, 77, 78, 79, 80, 81, 82, 83, 84, 85, 86, 87, 88, 89, 90, 91, 97, 101, 102, 103, 104, 105, 106, 107, 108, 109, 110, 111, 112, 113, 114, 115
induction, 35, 36, 37, 41

J

justice, 92, 96, 97, 98, 99, 100, 102, 107

K

Kandel, Eric, 2, 4, 6, 9, 15, 16, 17, 19

Kant, Immanuel, 7, 33, 34, 42, 87, 102
knowledge, vii, viii, 1, 2, 3, 4, 5, 6, 7, 9, 10, 14, 19, 23, 24, 26, 27, 28, 29, 33, 34, 35, 48, 56, 64, 67, 69, 101, 112, 113, 114

L

Livio, Mario, 76
Locke, John, 7, 25, 60, 63, 64, 65, 68
love, 89, 90, 104, 113

M

metaphor, 44, 77, 79, 87
metaphysics, viii, 7, 9, 32, 59, 60, 63, 70, 73, 85
meter, 78
Mill, John Stuart, 35, 36, 39, 43, 48
moral egalitarianism, 91, 101, 102

N

neuroscience, 2
Nietzsche, Friedrich, 26, 113
non-being, 19, 20, 27

O

ontology, viii, 7

P

particular, 9, 10, 12, 13, 14, 15, 18, 28, 31, 32, 54, 67, 87, 105, 112, 115
perception, 7, 8, 11, 18, 19, 20, 25, 29, 43, 52, 66, 67, 68, 88
Plato, 43, 44, 47, 48, 107
Plotinus, 13, 14, 60
proportion, 74, 75, 76, 77, 82, 92

Q

Quine, Willard Van Orman, 44

Index

R

reality as we know it, 1, 2, 8, 15, 16, 19, 20, 21, 22, 24, 26, 63, 64, 65, 66, 67, 68, 69, 70, 71, 87, 88, 89, 90, 112
reality in itself, 1, 2, 8, 15, 16, 19, 20, 21, 22, 23, 24, 26, 63, 64, 69, 70, 71, 85, 86, 112
reason, vii, viii, ix, 1, 2, 4, 6, 7, 8, 11, 13, 14, 15, 16, 18, 19, 20, 21, 22, 23, 26, 27, 28, 29, 30, 31, 32, 33, 34, 35, 36, 37, 39, 40, 42, 44, 45, 46, 48, 51, 52, 53, 54, 55, 59, 62, 63, 64, 67, 69, 71, 73, 76, 82, 83, 84, 85, 86, 88, 91, 97, 101, 104, 105, 106, 107, 108, 109, 110, 111, 112, 113, 114
rhyme, 78, 79
rhythm, 55, 80, 81, 85, 86, 98
Russell, Bertrand, 7, 13, 35, 36, 37, 38, 39, 60

S

Sartwell, Crispin, 74, 89
sensation, 7, 21, 28, 50, 65
sense-data, 4, 5
sensory experience, 2, 3, 7, 10, 11, 12, 16, 22, 26, 65, 66, 71, 112

Shaw, George Bernard, 101
similarity, 29, 36, 41, 42, 49, 50, 61
Spinoza, Baruch, 23
symmetry, 30, 74, 75, 76, 77, 90, 103

T

truth, viii, 2, 6, 9, 14, 35, 36, 56, 59, 60, 62, 63, 64, 70, 71, 73, 90, 98, 99, 103, 111, 113, 114, 118, 119

U

uniformity, 10, 11, 12, 13, 17, 18, 20, 21, 22, 26, 28, 36, 82, 84, 114
universal, 10, 12, 14, 20, 32, 33, 38, 44, 52, 77, 85, 86, 87, 88, 89, 101, 102, 103, 110, 112, 113, 115

V

Vitruvius, 74

W

Warren, Howard, 50, 51
Wölfflin, Heinrich, 74

www.ingramcontent.com/pod-product-compliance
Lightning Source LLC
Chambersburg PA
CBHW070643300426
44111CB00013B/2244